D0011473

THE
NEW DAD'S
SURVIVAL GUIDE

Also by Scott Mactavish

THE NEW DAD'S SURVIVAL GUIDE

Man-to-Man Advice for First-Time Fathers

SCOTT MACTAVISH

Little, Brown and Company

NEW YORK   BOSTON   LONDON

Copyright © 2003, 2005 by Scott Mactavish

All rights reserved. In accordance with the U.S. Copyright Act of 1976, the scanning, uploading, and electronic sharing of any part of this book without the permission of the publisher constitute unlawful piracy and theft of the author's intellectual property. If you would like to use material from the book (other than for review purposes), prior written permission must be obtained by contacting the publisher at permissions@hbgusa.com. Thank you for your support of the author's rights.

Little, Brown and Company
Hachette Book Group
1290 Avenue of the Americas, New York, NY 10104
www.littlebrown.com

First Edition: January 2005

Little, Brown and Company is a division of Hachette Book Group, Inc. The Little, Brown name and logo are trademarks of Hachette Book Group, Inc.

The publisher is not responsible for websites (or their content) that are not owned by the publisher.

This book is not intended as a substitute for medical advice from a physician. The reader should regularly consult a physician in all matters relating to health.

Library of Congress Cataloging-in-Publication Data
Mactavish, Scott.
    The new dad's survival guide : man-to-man advice for first-time fathers / Scott Mactavish.—1st ed.
        p. cm.
      ISBN 978-0-316-15995-1
    1. Children care. 2. Fathers. 3. Child rearing. 4. Parenting. I. Title.

RJ61.M355 2005
649'.122 — dc22   2004006991

20 19 18 17

LSC-C

Book Design by Robert G. Lowe

Printed in the United States of America

To Christy, Declan, and Kinzer

CONTENTS

MISSION CODES

NFU = new family unit

FPP = female parenting partner

BCF = be cool, fool

ATTENTION, NEW DADS!

YOU ARE ABOUT TO HAVE your world rocked.

You may think you know what's around the corner, but trust me, brother, you don't.

But don't worry; I've got your back.

I'm not an obstetrician, pediatrician, or psychologist. No, I'm just a dude who's been through it twice, and along the way I broke the code and absorbed numerous invaluable tricks and secrets that will help you prepare for the forthcoming physical, psychological, and emotional dragon ride called fatherhood.

I earned my stripes and I'll help you earn yours. Read on.

This manual covers a general time line that starts just before birth and continues through the first three months or so, with a few toddler tips thrown in. It's all about practical recommendations and is *not* meant to serve as medical advice. If you want a man's definition of a *pacifier* or advice on how to de-stress, you have the right book. If you're wondering if a pacifier is good for

x The New Dad's Survival Guide

your child, you should consult a medical professional — or at least someone a lot smarter than me. In fact, your mailman is probably better qualified to comment. Well, maybe not. Stick with your pediatrician.

After three or four months of fatherhood you'll be a pro; your pride will swell, and confidence will be yours. But for now, get ready for utter confusion and abject bewilderment; it has been so since the beginning of time and will continue to be so forever.

So grab your boots and strap on your helmet; the babies are coming.

Scott Mactavish

PREPARATIONS

YOUR MISSION ORDERS

ESTABLISH A PLAN and make provisions for your transformation from clueless civilian to competent father.

PREPARATIONS

LET'S DO THIS

SO YOU'RE GOING TO BE A DAD. Take it from me, there's nothing like it, bro. *Nothing*. Sure, you'll have a few bumps in the road, but just wait until you hold your son or see your daughter smile at you for the first time. They're moments you'll never ever forget. Believe it.

But until then, you have a steep learning curve, and that's where I come in. Before we start, however, let's clear up a few things:

First, I've tried to cut through the psychobabble and useless filler and get right to the straight dope. The contents herein are based on my own unique experiences and are by no means the final word. They are honest, though, and you can learn from my hard-earned successes and mistakes. Take it as one man's straight-up report from the trenches.

You'll also be relieved to know I spoke to dozens of doctors, nurses, new parents, midwives, mimes, Eskimos, and ninjas to get a full picture of new parenthood. They provided extra bonus information you'll enjoy wrapping your head around. So strap on your thinkin' cap, Gus.

When you see BCF, that means *be cool, fool*, borrowed from that profound and deeply moving contemporary philosopher Mr. T. Many of your anxieties and stresses, while valid, can be eliminated if you'll just take a deep breath and chill. You'll see what I mean.

And finally, this book is all about the birth and the following few months, when you'll be ramping up to full-on fatherhood. Though pregnancy is a whole different can of worms, there are a few important points you'll need to know in order to survive, and I've included them as well.

Enough said. Let's do this.

EARLY IN THE GAME . . .

IF IT'S EARLY in the pregnancy game for you — say, three months or so — pat yourself on the back for thinking ahead.

You may think that at this point most of the details are handled by the FPP (female parenting partner), and in some cases they are. But preparation is key, and to truly understand and enjoy the birth process (and, ultimately, the first few months of fatherhood), you should get involved now. Trust me on this, it won't kill you and you may actually have some fun.

GET TO KNOW YOUR OBSTETRICIAN (OB)

FIRST, LET'S CLEAR UP a couple of terms.

An *obstetrician* is a doctor who cares for pregnant women and their babies, from conception through delivery.

A *gynecologist* is a doctor who specializes in women's equipment.

Often doctors specialize in both areas and are referred to as OB/GYNs. (You've heard this before.)

By now your FPP has chosen the OB who will deliver your NFU (new family unit). At least I hope so, unless you're planning to do it yourself in the den, next to your recliner. If that's the case, I urge you to drop this book immediately and check yourself into a psychiatric ward, or at least get yourself some nice restaurant-grade salad tongs, just in case. Otherwise, you should be attending the periodic checkups along with the FPP, not only to get a status report on the NFU's progress but also to acquaint yourself with the OB and her or his staff.

They are very knowledgeable and accustomed to clueless fathers-to-be. And if you're lucky the way we were, they'll be very cool people, too.

"This will make you moody and temperamental."

During these visits the FPP is, of course, the star of the show. You sit quietly and listen and will probably be confused most of the time. This is natural and expected. However, you are allowed to pipe up with questions when they arise and you should get familiar with the key physiological terms: vagina (you already know this one, obviously), uterus, placenta, and umbilical, to name just a few. And for God's sake, no giggling. You need not attend every single appointment, but definitely go when a sonogram is scheduled, so you can see the NFU in its alien form. You may even get a picture to stick on the fridge.

A SPECIAL REPORT ON C-SECTIONS

CESAREAN SECTION (C-section, or "section" in nurse-speak) delivery is when the baby is unable to come out via the regular tunnel and must be taken out through an incision just above the pubic bone. Your OB may tell you months before the birth that a C-section is necessary, or in some cases, you may find out after the

FPP goes into labor and exhibits difficulties. Reasons for C-section include low levels of fluids in the womb, a distressed fetus, or health problems with the mom, such as high blood pressure.

Even if your FPP is healthy and the sonograms indicate "all's well," it would be wise to familiarize yourself with the C-section protocol, just in case. Many OB offices have books and videos that explain the process and prepare you for the procedure, should it become necessary. And if it is, don't sweat too much; it's a very common operation. Upward of 50 percent of deliveries are C-sections.

More about C-sections later.

DRUGS AND STUFF

NOW IS THE TIME to discuss the different types of drugs available during delivery (for her, not you, although you may want something after you see a head pop out of your FPP's nether regions). You should ask about epidurals and analgesics and the pros and cons associated with each. Of course, it's her decision, but you'll definitely want to know what's going on when they stick a needle in your lovely girl's spinal column and start pumping in strange fluids. (See the Glossary for an explanation of the epidural.)

It's beyond the scope of this book to recommend any type of drug, but I've seen an epidural turn a snarling, thrashing alligator into a kitten in the span of five minutes. You do the math.

EDUCATION = SERENITY

THERE ARE FEW TIPS more important than the one I'm about to lay on you. You may resist and go kicking and screaming, but believe me, on the big day you will be glad you went. Most obstetricians offer these classes or can refer you to a good teacher. Here goes:

CRITICAL SURVIVAL TIP

Attend childbirth education classes with the FPP. Doing so will prevent a major freak-out when a human pops out of your FPP's private parts, as well as preparing you for your role as a birthing coach.

The classes usually take place one evening a week for two months and are attended by eight or ten couples, all about as far along as you in the pregnancy cycle. The classes cover everything from the actual mechanics of the birthing process (which is pretty damn cool, actually) to breathing exercises to postpartum psychology.

But mainly you learn how to be a birthing coach.

Your role as birthing coach is to keep your FPP as comfortable as possible and handle the logistics outside the birthing room, such as calling grandparents and fetching ice chips during the labor process.

"I coached ice dancing at my college."

The breathing exercises are very important, and you *will* use them in the delivery room. Pay special attention because the FPP will need your help while your son or daughter squirms out through the exit chute.

You also learn how and when to give proper back-rubs, the mechanics of the womb (very cool, incidentally), relaxation techniques, and when to hold the FPP's legs, among other topics.

CRITICAL SURVIVAL TIP

Pay special attention to the breathing exercises. You *will* use them during the delivery.

READ NOW, REJOICE LATER

AS YOUR NFU DEVELOPS, he begins to pick up sounds from outside his current quarters at the Hotel FPP. He hears music, voices, dogs barking, and horns honking. In fact, he hears a muffled version of nearly everything you hear. Your voice becomes especially familiar to him, and on the big day, when he is jerked from his warm womb with a view and placed on a cold, bright table and you talk to him face-to-face for the first time, he will recognize your voice and *it will calm him down* and you will remember that one moment for the rest of your life. Believe it.

You can establish early communication with your NFU by reading to him through the FPP's belly. Though it may seem odd at first, you will get the hang of it and he will respond with kicks and punches — his way of telling you, "Hey, I like *Sports Illustrated*, keep it up, big guy." And you can read anything; he doesn't care: the *York Times*, a magazine, a children's book . . . as long as he hears your voice, he's happy. However, it may be wise to avoid any type of adult material, as the FPP may swat the back of your head if you tell the NFU the one about the blonde, the priest, and the chicken.

One very cool residual effect of womb reading is kids' response to books as they grow. Aside from his soccer ball, my NFU's favorite possessions are books. At three months he would instantly calm down when read to and at six months knew how to flip through a book from front to back. (Hell, yes, I'm a proud dad!)

FINANCES

SEEMS SIMPLE ENOUGH. Just budget for one more person, who probably won't eat much anyway, right?

I weep for you, brother, if that's your outlook. Your whole financial life is about to get flipped — but with a little planning, you can get through it just fine. The following are a few of the issues you'll need to attend to:

1. Insurance. Time to add baby and watch the premium jump. If you're covered by your job, and I hope you are, make certain pediatric care is part of your coverage. Also get yourself a nice life insurance policy covering the family in case you get smoked (God forbid). A thirty-year-old guy can purchase a term life insurance policy offering $500,000 in coverage for about $200 a year.

You are about to make your insurance agent very happy.

CRITICAL SURVIVAL TIP

Check your health insurance to ensure that all of your expenses are covered, including the anesthesiologist (if the FPP receives an epidural), obstetrician, hospital stay, aftercare, etc. Virtually everything in and around the hospital is expensive, so check the policy closely to avoid nasty surprises.

2. Will. Get yourself a good lawyer to write up a will, or to cut the costs, buy a software program and do it yourself. (You'll have to have it witnessed and notarized.) Either way, be sure your assets have a place to go other than probate, for probate is a pain in the assets.

Don't you wish.

3. College savings. I don't need to explain this one. Anyone who's been to college in the past ten years knows what the costs are like. And when your NFU is ready eighteen years from now, who knows what kind of hellish tuition bill will arrive in one of those annoying envelopes with plastic windows. Better to plan with a competent financial adviser now than to sell the boat later. Oh, and if you aspire to enroll the NFU in private school in a few years, be advised that the tuition for the better schools matches the gross national product of several small Caribbean nations.

And that's just for textbooks!

CRITICAL SURVIVAL TIP

The miracle of compound interest should be fully exploited when choosing a college savings plan. For example:

$5,000 @ 6% interest × 18 years = $14,271.70

That's if you don't touch it. It would obviously be much more if you added $1,000 annually for the eighteen years or if you found a higher interest rate. Also, be sure to discuss tax benefits with your financial planner when setting up a college savings plan.

---

4. Baby gear, food, and clothing. Dear God, women love baby gear. Yes, much of it is necessary, but be prepared: every bit of your beer money on onesies, sippy cups, binkies, and bouncy chairs. (Don't worry, I explain all of these in the Glossary.) Baby does indeed need a new pair of shoes, so be prepared to fill every single free inch of your home with baby paraphernalia. And forget about the beer money, you won't have time to enjoy it anyway.

5. Transportation. Go ahead, grab the Kleenex. You will soon trade in your pickup for a minivan, and there's not a damn thing you can do about it.

Say hello to your new set of wheels
and good-bye to your manhood.

THE PEDIATRICIAN

YOU SHOULD FIND a good pediatrician a few months before the birth. Your best bet is to get a referral from friends, relatives, or your OB. Get a few names and set up interviews at their offices if possible. Obviously, you want a physician with great credentials, reputation, and education. But you also want a doctor you click with on a more personal level. Why? Because the first time your NFU comes down with a fever or the croup, you'll freak out and need someone you can trust on the other end of the phone at 3:00 A.M. Pediatricians, like OBs, are a unique breed and are accustomed to wigged-out parents who call at midnight or burst through the clinic door with wild eyes and a feverish baby in tow. It's good to have a physician with an even temperament; he or she will keep you calm.

Here are a few questions to ask at the interview:

- Are there other doctors in the practice? Who will take over if my primary physician is away?
- How many offices are in the practice, where are they, what are the hours, etc.?
- Will the doctor visit the NFU as a newborn?
- What is the protocol for emergency calls, late-night calls, emergency visits, etc.?
- Does the office have walk-in hours, or is it appointment-only?
- How does the billing work in relation to my insurance policy? (Take an insurance card to the meeting.)
- Who are the nurses and assistants?

But ask any other questions that chap you.

CRITICAL SURVIVAL TIP

Once you choose a pediatrician, put the office numbers on speed dial on all of your phones, including your cell. You will inevitably need it while driving and don't want to crash or break the law trying to find the number.

COUNTDOWN: ONE MONTH TO D-DAY

OKAY, SO NOW YOU'RE EDUCATED and the paperwork is done.

Get ready, big guy, it's party time. You've been through eight months of pregnancy (fun, ain't it?) and birthing classes, and now Junior's 'bout to break on out.

Or maybe you've spent the better part of three years trudging through the adoption process, chopping away paperwork like vines in the jungle, and now your new recruit is on the bus home.

Either way, Slappy, your life's about to change big-time, and no matter what you anticipate, it will be a thousand times more intense than you ever imagined. The lows are low, and the highs are better than any drug on earth.

Sure, you're nervous now, but just wait until that little guy wraps his hand around your finger or smiles up at you with those gnarly gums. Your heart will break a million times, in a good way, and you'll forever be Daddy and you'll wear your stripes proudly. But there are a few more cats to skin — nasty, screeching cats with claws like razors. So let's break out the Ka-Bars and get busy, it's almost *"go" time!*

PREPPING THE QUARTERS

YOUR FPP HAS very specific ideas how the nursery should look. (I always thought a nursery was a place where they grew fancy plants that cost too much.) In fact, she has been secretly planning the layout of this sacred room since she was twelve (about the same time the wedding plans started). It will do you no good to resist, so just go with the flow.

The following are a few major pieces of gear you should pick up and install in the nursery. They can be found online or at a nearby retailer. Just ask your FPP: she has memorized every baby store within a fifty-mile radius and probably knows the telephone numbers by heart.

CRITICAL SURVIVAL TIP

Women love to throw baby showers. And no, it's not some weird ritual involving soggy infants. It's really a party where they get together and "shower" the prospective mom with gifts. Make certain your FPP's friends facilitate this evolution so that you can rack up the free loot.

- changing table (this can be a dresser)
- crib
- gear shelf, for diapers, wipes, etc. (should go next to changing table)
- rocker

- diaper pail
- stereo/boom box

Ka-ching! Bye-bye, season tickets; hello, diaper pail!

CRITICAL SURVIVAL TIP

You can save tons of dough by hunting for baby gear at yard sales and consignment shops or by asking friends. If you do buy it secondhand, be sure to sanitize it thoroughly, especially the plastic items. Be advised: the FPP may resist this, as shopping for new baby gear is a sacred, time-honored rite of passage. Also be sure to check *Consumer Reports* to ensure that your new bargain has not been recalled.

There are tons of small items to consider as well, and it's a pretty sure bet the FPP has most of these covered:

- mobile
- musical crib toy
- stuffed animals
- night-lights
- humidifier
- dehumidifier
- A&D ointment

> ## CRITICAL SURVIVAL TIP
> If you live in a two-story house, set up two separate changing stations, one upstairs and one down. The last thing a sore post-delivery FPP needs is a frequent hike up the steps.

THE CIRCUMCISION

THIS COULD BE A BOOK all by itself, one I sure as hell don't want to read. How many men really want to think about having the willie skinned? Imagine if you were lying in a warm, quiet bed and strange giants walked in, held you down, and snipped your dink? Fact is, you probably experienced this but are repressing it, because in today's society most baby boys have the procedure done. It's a personal choice based on a number of factors, such as religion, culture, tradition, and hygiene, and is best discussed with your doctor. You need to line it up a month or so before D-Day to allow the pediatrician time to schedule the procedure. (If you wait until the big day to learn the NFU's gender, you should have the snipper standing by, just in case it is a boy and you want to trim his little turtleneck.)

Quite honestly, this section is giving me the heebie-jeebies, so let's get on with it. If you have a boy:

- Ask your pediatrician ahead of time about the procedure. Does he or she have a recommendation for a specialist? Or does he or she do the procedure?

- The procedure takes place shortly after birth, probably the next day. Welcome to the world, little man!
- As soon as you get home, he will pee and the scream will sound like a smoke detector and you may even cry right along with him when you see the raw unit.
- The doctor will give you aftercare instructions and I will not.
- He will recover and play with his tool, and you will be proud.

"This just in! Circumcision hurts like hell!"

THE HOSPITAL — RECONNAISSANCE

GO NOW — GET IN the car and drive to the hospital. Turn around, come back home, and repeat the trip until it's committed to memory. Then find an alternative route and memorize it, too. You probably won't need it, but better safe than sorry, Ace.

Once you have the route under control, set up a time to tour the hospital with your FPP. Most hospitals will give you a tour of the facility if you wipe the mustard off your chin and ask real nice. It's important to tour the birthing room and surrounding areas, as you want to know where the cafeteria is in relation to the room. You should also run recon in the labor/delivery ward to find ice machines and towel storage as well as the nurses' station. Also check to see if a TV is available in case labor is a marathon. In case you haven't heard this already, labor can run twenty-four hours or longer, so be prepared.

PACKING FOR THE HOSPITAL

CRITICAL SURVIVAL TIP
You will be an absolute hero if you bring the FPP's favorite pillow.

WHEN IT GETS CLOSE TO "GO" TIME, pack a bag and set it near the door. You should include the following items:

- snacks, in case the cafeteria sucks and the vending machine is out of bear claws
- books, magazines, and, if possible, a Game Boy. *Caution:* Turn the sound off, or a very large maternity nurse will lay a Jackie Chan on your ass.
- boom box with the FPP's favorite CDs. Some hospitals allow music during the birth, and it's a very cool touch. Be sure to ask first, however, or you may encounter the same nurse from the previous point.
- snacks, especially bear claws
- toothbrushes/toothpaste for everyone
- bathrobe and gown for the FPP
- lip balm (unflavored)
- warm socks and slippers (nonskid preferred)

- camera, film, batteries
- video camera (Get the FPP's permission before filming her nether regions.)
- a change of clothes for everybody: you, the FPP, and the NFU. That's right, you need to take an NFU outfit for the ride home: undershirt, sleeper, blanket, and hat. This is when reality starts to take hold.
- baby carrier/car seat. You need to carry baby out in an approved baby carrier, preferably a car seat. See the Glossary for details.

CRITICAL SURVIVAL TIP

You will be in the birthing room for the delivery, then in a room on the maternity ward for the recovery. Now is the time to arrange for a private room, if your insurance covers it. You may be crying like a four-year-old girl when you see your NFU, so believe me, a private room is good. Many hospitals and insurance plans require you to leave after two days of recovery, so be certain to check in advance and plan accordingly.

"I was *not* crying! I had an eyelash in my eye!"

THE REINFORCEMENTS

YOU NEED TO ARRANGE for help at home after the big day. When you arrive home and the little gal/guy hurls for the first time, it is a good idea to have an experienced baby wrangler standing by to keep you from hurling, too.

CRITICAL SURVIVAL TIP

If you're lucky enough to have the new grandmothers nearby, invite them to stay back-to-back weeks to help with the NFU. This gives you fourteen days to assimilate to your new life.

If grandmas aren't available, talk to your OB about aftercare nursing services. You may be able to have your own in-home nurse for a few days after the birth. (Be prepared to pay, however.) Childcare's just one issue. You'll be in shock the first few days and will need help with cooking and cleaning as well. The FPP may be very tired and sore, and Grandma will be an absolute lifesaver. Plus she'll be so thrilled to be with the NFU that you may actually get a nap in. It's smart to schedule this now to ensure that flight arrangements and hide-a-beds are in order, unless she plans to sleep with you. Let's move along.

"Hello, dear! Shall I put my things in your room?"

CRITICAL SURVIVAL TIP

Have frozen meals in the freezer so you can concentrate on the NFU and FPP when you arrive home. The microwave is your friend.

YOUR FURRY FRIENDS

NO, NOT THE GUYS you played ball with in college. Your pets. Be sure to leave them extra food in case you're stuck at the hospital for an extended period of time. And also be prepared for them to act neurotic when the NFU comes home. Up until now, they have received all of the attention, and they may just act out when you start baby-talking to the NFU.

CRITICAL SURVIVAL TIP

Hold your pets firmly and let them view the baby from a few feet away. They will be puzzled at first but will eventually calm down once they get used to the NFU.

You may want to keep hungry pets away from the NFU.

THE BIRTH

YOUR MISSION ORDERS

WELCOME YOUR NFU into the world without suffering a major anxiety attack, cardiac infarction, or other bodily meltdown.

THE BIRTH

LET'S GET RIGHT TO IT. The big day is coming, and it's one you'll remember for the rest of your life.

In order to survive, however, you need to know more than just breathing exercises and cord cutting. In fact, one of the most stressful evolutions of the birth day is learning to navigate the hospital while still attending to the FPP. But because you are squared away and did your reconnaissance (see previous chapter), you have your notes at hand and know the location of all critical areas in relation to the labor/delivery floor.

Be advised that labor could take a while and you may spend the better part of the next couple of days wringing your hands, pacing the floor, and being utterly confused by your FPP.

To relieve some stress and make the wait bearable, I suggest you make the rounds of the labor/delivery floor and introduce yourself to every staff member you encounter, from doctors and nurses to cleaning staff and volunteers. If you have questions, ask.

Hospital staffers, especially those assigned to the labor/delivery wards, are extremely knowledgeable and will be happy to answer your questions. And for God's sake, be nice to them; they tend to be very kind people and are accustomed to sweaty, saucer-eyed fathers-to-be who need an extra pillow or an Italian ice. They will bend over backward to help you unless, of course, you're a tool, in which case they may direct you to the nearest bedpan-cleaning room. You will be stressed, and that's okay. Just mind your manners. BCF.

THE PROTOCOL

YOUR EXPERIENCE MAY VARY depending on major factors such as C-section vs. natural birth, complications, etc., and if any extenuating circumstances exist, your health-care provider should prep you ahead of time.

Assuming the NFU is taking the traditional vaginal-birth route, the following is a recommended course of action:

- Arrive at hospital, check in, and decompress. Breathe deeply. BCF.
- Square away the room. Situate the boom box within reach of the FPP. Make her as comfortable as possible; it could be a long wait.
- Introduce yourself to the nurses on duty. They come and go regularly and are not scared of expectant fathers. Be nice to them: they are in charge. (You may have to do this again at the shift change, depending on the length of labor.)
- Run a recon mission through the immediate area. Find the nurses' station, ice bin, and elevators. You also want to know where the cafeteria and gift shop are located, as well as an outdoor area where you can use your cell phone.
- Call the relatives with a status report.
- BCF.

CRITICAL SURVIVAL TIP

Some birthing centers make cots available to expectant fathers who choose to stick around for marathon labors. Trust me, they are a quantum leap more comfortable than the bedside chairs provided in the birthing rooms. Ask the shift nurse if a cot is available and offer to help retrieve it.

Now that the perimeter is secure, you should attend to the FPP until told otherwise. Trust me, this is not the time to tighten up e-mail on your laptop or catch a ball-game score on TV. Once labor starts, it can be a grueling, painful experience for her, and she needs you there to rub her back and coach her through the pain. Be prepared for anything: she may want a backrub, or she may threaten your life if you touch her. Regardless, it is probably too early in the game for her to receive drugs, and she will tell you exactly what she wants.

Regarding drugs: as mentioned previously, this is something that you decide beforehand based on the advice given by your health-care provider, as there is risk involved. I can comment only on my experience, and let me tell you, brother, that epidural is one astounding invention. My FPP had been in labor for eighteen hours and she was not a happy camper. In fact, if I got within reach, she would yank the hair off my arms or worse, depending on my proximity and the severity of the contractions. She'd been given a mild analgesic and it worked to an extent, but nothing like the epidural. Once they poked that needle in her spine

(yup, the spine) and injected the drug, the pain sub-
sided down below and life was calm again.

Before the epidural . . .   . . . and after

CRITICAL SURVIVAL TIP

Hospital-room television sets have speakers in the bedrails,
which means the FPP can hear but you cannot. Check the
surrounding waiting areas, as they have televisions with
regular speakers in the event you need to sneak off and
check the sports scores . . . I mean, news. Check the *news.*

So now you know what to expect at the hospital.
Let's get on to the birth.

THE BIRTH
OR
IT'S "GO" TIME . . . LABOR, PANIC, AND
THAT FUNKY MUCUS PLUG

THE BIG DAY is here.

0630 ZULU TIME — NFU ARRIVAL DAY

YOU'VE BEEN WAITING nine months and your senses are fine-tuned, your wits razor-sharp. The bags are packed, the route to the hospital has been memorized, and "Ain't no baby gonna make me panic," you tell yourself. Confidence is yours. This fatherhood thing, you say, is a piece of cake. Then she says it:

"I think my water broke!"

You jump from the bed and land on jelly knees. Your cool veneer cracks like an eggshell; the nine months of mental preparation suddenly seems woefully inadequate. Your heart races, breathing accelerates, and your pupils dilate like Frisbees. Your instincts take over and you scream death threats at the cat as you stumble down the stairs with suitcases in hand. You trip over the dog as you rush to start the car, all while your FPP slowly, methodically speed dials the doctor, applies lipstick, feeds the pets, and issues orders as she shuffles toward the car, a picture of calm, determined fortitude. It enrages you; panic should be a shared burden. You ease her into the car, run around to your side, and crack a rib as you throw open the door with staggering, adrenaline-charged force. Your FPP rolls her eyes and tells you to relax. You do not relax. You speed off, throw gravel against the neighbor's house, and run directly into a traffic jam. She tells you that everything is fine. You bruise both of your hands banging on the steering wheel, and your vocal cords nearly rupture as you scream profanities at the garbage truck in front of you. Your FPP turns on soothing music; you break off the radio knob and demand silence as you try to concentrate. She tries to calm you, and her Zen-like state further enrages you. You then lay on the horn for forty-five seconds while a school bus executes a three-point turn directly in your path. The schoolchildren stare at your saucer-size eyes and untamed hair and laugh as you chew off all of your fingernails. Seconds turn into hours. You are convinced that the baby is halfway out and that Stu, the sweaty bread truck guy from Hoboken, is going to deliver your NFU on the side of the highway, and you begin to hyperventilate. Finally there's a break in the traffic, and you destroy the sound barrier as you careen into the hospital emergency area. You help your FPP to the reception desk, and a calm, apathetic administrator asks for your insurance information, at which time you may begin to tremble with rage. It's then that a kindly, knowledgeable maternity nurse appears to escort your FPP to the maternity ward and you are told to retrieve the bags from the car and to relax, everything is fine. You finally breathe and weep with relief, watching your FPP smile and wave as she walks away.

Over her shoulder she whispers, "Be cool, fool."

Or not.

If you do your homework now, attend the childbirth classes, and generally educate yourself about the whole process, then labor won't sneak up on you and knock your breath out. You've already taken care of the preparations described earlier, so let's get to the nitty-gritty of what you need to know as labor coach.

CRITICAL SURVIVAL TIP

For the first stages of labor it is only you and the FPP in the room, with occasional visits from the nurses. The doctor pops in from time to time but doesn't stick around until Junior is ready to make his appearance. If you have questions or concerns, be sure to address them when the doc stops in.

LABOR

THIS CAN BE one confusing can of worms, Jack. There are stages of labor, and within those stages you have phases.

Thanks to Shirley Griffith at Maternal Fetal Care in Stamford, Connecticut, for breaking it down.

I. FIRST STAGE OF LABOR

Phase One
Prelabor/false labor (on and off for several days)

Phase Two
Early labor (typically eight to twelve hours)

Phase Three
Active labor (usually four to six hours)

Phase Four
Transition (typically half an hour to two and a half hours)

II. SECOND STAGE OF LABOR
The pushing starts here (average one to three hours for first baby)

III. THIRD STAGE OF LABOR
Delivery of afterbirth/placenta and repair episiotomies if required
Warning! Do not watch any of this unless you have a great therapist!

IV. POSTPARTUM
Expect a six-to-eight-week recovery time

CRITICAL SURVIVAL TIP
During labor you are waiting for the cervix to dilate. In man-speak, there's a little gasketlike gadget that slowly opens and lets the NFU slide into the birth canal. It starts at 1 centimeter (cm) and opens up to 10 cm. When you hear the doctor say the FPP's at 8 cm, you know it's almost showtime.

And this is how each of the stages breaks down. Take note: the first stage is a little confusing because it has four subphases.

FIRST STAGE OF LABOR

The first stage of labor has four phases.

Phase One: Prelabor/false labor

It may continue off and on for several hours or even days before true, early labor begins. It varies from woman to woman, so it's way unpredictable. Only 10 to 12 percent actually experience water breakage (also known as "spontaneous rupture of membranes") during this phase. The FPP knows that this stage has started by the onset of such symptoms as a vague, nagging backache, cramps, unusual bursts of energy, and several soft bowel movements. (Go ahead, Skippy! Have a look at the stool! Is it soft?) At this stage, the uterus is "practicing" for real labor. The cervix is beginning to ripen, which means it's getting thinner and more anterior in the FPP's pelvis. (To this day I can't look at a "ripened" apple without shivering.)

"Did someone say 'apples'?"

CRITICAL SURVIVAL TIP

You are so ready for the big event that you may be mistaking indigestion, fatigue, or overexertion for labor. It's important to keep cool now and watch for other signs that indicate the onset of the real thing.

YOUR MISSION ORDERS

- As labor coach, you are justifiably nervous or anxious. But just imagine what the FPP feels like, with a human sliding down the exit chute. Suck it up and make her comfortable.
- If she is well rested, try taking her for a walk or help her take a warm bath.
- Most important, keep her well hydrated with Gatorade or other clear liquids.
- Keep her energy up by giving her healthy snacks. Carbohydrates are easier to digest, so no bacon cheeseburgers at this point. Ask your doctor for advice on snacks for this phase.

CRITICAL SURVIVAL TIP

Your FPP will be going through a whole laundry list of aches, pains, cramps, and spasms. You will be an absolute hero if you offer backrubs on a consistent basis.

Phase Two: Early Labor

This generally lasts eight to twelve hours, but it can vary. Usually in this phase the water breaks and bad cramping starts. Contraction pain is felt only in the lower abdomen and lasts thirty to sixty seconds. Sleep is nearly impossible for her, but catnapping may be an option. As this phase continues, the length and severity of contractions increase and get closer together. Guess what? "True labor" has most likely begun. The cervix is dilating, and Junior is moving closer to the escape hatch. He will probably break free within the next twenty-four hours!

CRITICAL SURVIVAL TIP

She may lose her "mucus plug" at this point. Ask your doctor to explain this in advance, as you may go into shock if you see it by accident.

YOUR MISSION ORDERS

- Distract the FPP with games, television, or armpit farts.
- Help her rest, keep up the fluids, and rub her back.
- Try a warm shower.
- *Now* is the time to place the bags near the front door and notify relatives and employers.
- Call the doctor now and put him or her on notice.
- Remind her to pee.
- Encourage her.

Phase Three: Active Labor

Contractions are longer and stronger, and the FPP is completely distracted and unable to speak. She may have "bloody show," which as you know by now are a few small spots of bright red blood. She may have nausea and may vomit; but of course so might you, depending on how well you handle pressure. If her water hasn't broken by now, get ready for the gates to open. The FPP may now ask for and receive a painkiller or anesthesia. She may also ask for ice chips or other clear liquid.

CRITICAL SURVIVAL TIP

It's during this evolution that the FPP may be offered an epidural. Be advised that the epidural can turn a writhing, cursing FPP into a giddy schoolgirl in about ten minutes. It is highly recommended that you discuss this decision weeks in advance with your OB.

YOUR MISSION ORDERS

- Help the FPP adjust her breathing technique.
- Help her relax by giving verbal directions: "Come on, loosen those knees."
- Make her laugh if you can. Good luck.
- She may try to walk to relieve the pain. Allow her to lean on you.
- If you're not already at the hospital, get crackin', Ace. Avoid bumps and rush-hour traffic.

Phase Four: Transition

Contractions are very strong and very close together. To the FPP it feels like one long, agonizing contraction. This phase can last up to two and a half hours. The cervix is dilating from 8 cm to 10 cm, which makes it "fully dilated." The NFU is squirming through the cervix into the vagina as if it were a tight turtleneck. It is *almost* time to start pushing.

YOUR MISSION ORDERS

- BCF. You are no good to the FPP or NFU during an anxiety attack. They are in good hands.
- Use a cool cloth to wipe her brow.
- Continue breathing exercises to help her relax. Slow, deep, rhythmic.
- Do *not* encourage her to push even if she feels like it. Call the nurse.
- Do whatever it takes to help her relax.
- Be patient. She is most likely cursing you at this point and may possibly even be threatening divorce. Don't worry, bro, she doesn't mean it.

SECOND STAGE OF LABOR
Time to push!

Not you, man, her!

She now feels a great deal of pressure in the rectum, as if she needs to move her bowels. In fact, many women do let a little mud slip out. It is strongly suggested that you not crack a joke if this happens, or you may be wearing said mud or pulling her fingernails out of your arm.

For women having their first baby, this phase averages about two hours, depending on the baby's size and Mom's pushing technique.

So, What's Going On In There?
The NFU is exiting the uterus and heading for the exit door, aka the vagina. (And you always thought it was

an entrance!) The uterus is contracting and pushing down, and the FPP is crunching her ab muscles, all in an effort to coax Junior into the daylight.

What's Going On Out Here?

The FPP is on her back, with her legs up in stirrups. The nurses are prepping the room, and the doctor is now standing by, most likely very calm and confident. In fact, the doc may not even don his or her smock and gloves until seconds before the delivery. You see that the nurses have their routine down to a science and you feel relieved. Meanwhile, Mom is pushing and cursing and spitting, and you need to help.

YOUR MISSION ORDERS

- Put on her favorite CD.
- Offer ice chips and wipe her brow with a cool cloth.
- Emphasize the breathing exercises you have practiced.
- In a soothing voice, remind her to relax.
- Encourage her to rest between pushes.
- Hold her legs and support the back of her neck. (A nurse is there to assist, too.)
- Cheer her on. She is frustrated and in pain and may even want to give up. It is up to you to rally her spirits.

My God, a Head!

So it all leads up to this. The classes, the shopping trips, the special diets, the raging emotional outbursts for no reason . . . they're all things of the past because . . .

It's baby time.

So now the FPP has her legs up and you're holding one thigh while you support the back of her neck with your other hand. You're cheering her on while she sweats, puffs, cries, and begs you to let her go home. The doctor shrugs on a smock and snaps the gloves while the nurse spreads out sterile cloth around the landing zone. Another nurse is issuing gentle orders to the FPP, and the doc may offer you a sneak peek of the NFU's head. (Don't lose track of the leg you're supposed to be holding.) The doc is giving a play-by-play as the baby's head starts to exit the vagina, and you are equal parts elated and freaked out. You see your child, albeit only the crown of his head, and you feel a wave of emotion build. The doc continues the color commentary, and your FPP continues to hiss, grunt, and shriek.

And suddenly, with little warning, your NFU pops right out and into the doc's hands. He is bloody and covered in a waxy white substance and is the most handsome kid you've ever seen in your life. His head may be cone-shaped or flat on one side and his eyes glued shut, but you don't care. It's your son!

The world starts to move in real time again. After hours of waiting and anticipation, the room explodes with activity.

The medical team quickly clears the baby's breathing passages and gets him breathing (no cartoonish butt slapping in this century). It is now that you hear his pipes for the first time, and the FPP is laughing and crying simultaneously.

And now the doc offers you a pair of surgical scissors and you cut the umbilical cord — an event you will never ever forget for as long as you live.

CRITICAL SURVIVAL TIP

Cutting the Umbilical Cord

- Hold the FPP's leg and cheer her on while baby wiggles through the last few inches of tunnel.
- The doctor plucks him from the hidey-hole and clears his airway, then clamps off the umbilical cord, which looks like light blue tubing.
- When the doc hands you the scissors, shake off your stunned look and snip through the cord, which is very delicate and gives easily.

The stunned look returns to your face momentarily, until you realize you're a father, at which time you may laugh, cry, scream, faint, or any combination thereof.

From here, you are mere moments from holding your new favorite person.

You did it!

"Don't worry, you won't blow chunks. And I should know!"

CRITICAL SURVIVAL TIP

Your NFU will look just like an alien for her first few minutes of freedom. Depending on her trip down the fun chute, her head may be oddly shaped and she may be a strange color, perhaps blue, pink, or very white. She may be covered in a waxy white substance or blood. For God's sake, this is definitely a time to BCF. And don't worry: the nurses will clean her up and she'll be beautiful. And if she has a cone head . . . don't worry, time will round it out just fine.

Once the cord is cut, the NFU gets cleaned up, wrapped in a baby blanket, and handed to the FPP or placed on a special table with a heat lamp, not unlike the cheeseburger bin at Burger King. He also gets a snappy baby-size tuke (a knit toboggan hat, for those of you south of the line), and you are encouraged to meet your NFU. You go to him and gently touch him, and he may grab your finger. And when you speak to him, he knows your voice instantly.

And you may break down and cry like a three-year-old girl with bees in her shirt. Be advised that you will not be mocked, as the medical team is accustomed to seeing new fathers break like straw in a tornado, so go ahead, bro, it's been a long day.

Speaking of long days, back at the table o' fun, the FPP and doc are working on the . . .

THIRD STAGE OF LABOR

You as the dad need only know that you don't want to be around for this one.

The placenta (afterbirth) is separating from the uterine wall and will soon pop out into a tray held by the nurse. This can take five minutes or an hour, but count on thirty minutes. The doc is waiting patiently; once it is ejected, he or she will patch up the FPP's privates.

Once that's attended to, the NFU may be handed over to the FPP (and you, too, of course) for some bonding. You spend a few minutes with him and are mesmerized.

Inevitably, he must be taken to the nursery for measurements, cleaning, and perhaps testing (hearing, etc.).

It is difficult to watch him go with the nurse, but go he must. Just BCF; you'll see him soon.

POSTGAME

After the delivery the FPP is taken to the maternity floor for recovery time, and the NFU is safely squared away in the nursery.

At this point you hit the wall. Exhaustion is overwhelming, and you should go home for some rack time — that is, if you can drive safely. The NFU is in good hands, and the FPP needs sleep worse than you do. So go on home, Dad, and get some sleep. You'll have plenty of time to play with the NFU tomorrow. Don't forget to kiss the FPP good-bye . . . she's been through hell and deserves some reverence. (Don't dare forget the flowers on your next visit, Slappy. What are you, nuts?)

CRITICAL SURVIVAL TIP

Hospital visiting hours for new dads are pretty liberal. As long as you're cool (BCF), the hospital staff will more than likely allow you to see the NFU as much as you like. Be advised: he's had a rough few days as well and needs sleep as badly as you do.

GETTING ACQUAINTED

NOW THE FUN STUFF STARTS. For the next couple of days you and the FPP get a mini crash course in NFU mechanics from the hospital staff. Within seventy-two hours or so, you will be alone with Junior and panic will set in. Just BCF and pay attention; they tell you everything you need to know to fly solo with the NFU.

CIRCUMCISION

SORRY, I KNOW WE COVERED this already. But you need to know specifics.

It happens pretty quickly after the birth, within a day or two. If you even have to ask if he'll be in pain, then try this: take a cheese grater to your sausage and wrap it in gauze, then strap on one of those adult diapers and pee in it. You'll understand why he squeals like a stuck swine.

The doctor will instruct you in how to care for the little guy. It usually involves the application of ointment and gauze for a few days, until the redness and pain dissipate. Go easy, it's tender down there.

FPP RECOVERY DRILL

SO NOW YOU'RE A DAD and you've been home to rest.

The new mom is busy recovering for the next few days as well, with at least one of them in the hospital. She gets to see the NFU as much as she likes and spends much of her downtime sleeping.

This is also a huge bonding time for the three of you, so visit as much as possible.

You also start feeding the little guy, and if the FPP has chosen the breast over the bottle, you see her in action for the first time. More about this later . . . Just try not to laugh or gasp when you see the NFU latch on for breakfast; the results could be painful.

Whether you plan to feed the NFU by boob or bottle, you need to learn how to do it properly. The mechanics are simple enough, but there are a few tricks your nurse will demonstrate for you. If you have questions, ask.

"Hee-hee . . . he's eating straight from the cow . . . *owww!*"

THE DISCHARGE

AS MENTIONED PREVIOUSLY, your hospital and insurance company have discharge policies in place, more than likely forty-eight hours from the birth.

Once this is determined, you need to bring a change of clothes for the NFU and possibly the FPP, as well as the car seat, which will be used to carry the NFU down from the room.

CRITICAL SURVIVAL TIP

Let the nurses help you strap the NFU into the car seat. You will be nervous the first few times you handle your daughter, and they will demonstrate the proper method.

You pack up and carry down the FPP's belongings (be prepared to make a few trips) and pull the car around to the appropriate exit.

Meanwhile, the FPP is signing out and receiving last-minute health instructions from the nurses. She is also covering up the NFU (who, by the way, looks damn cute in his outfit and tuke) and saying good-bye to the awesome staff on the maternity floor.

She hobbles into a wheelchair, and an orderly escorts her down to meet you.

You greet your family (say it with me: *fam-il-y*) at the door and very cautiously place the NFU and his car seat in the car. You also point out the corny yellow window sign that says BABY ON BOARD, and the FPP laughs.

You help her into the car and drive off, happy to be heading home. Be advised, you will instinctively drive very slowly and scream the f-word at anyone who drives up on your back bumper. The FPP will say, "BCF."

POSTPARTUM DEPRESSION

I'M INCLUDING THIS in the "Birth" chapter because it can kick in literally at postpartum, that is, when the NFU is born, or a few days thereafter.

PPD is a *beaucoup* serious condition that can have a devastating effect on the FPP. Characterized by extreme sadness, anxiety, or even anger, the condition can be seen in about 10 percent of new moms. Sometimes called "the baby blues," it typically goes away after a few days. However, in severe cases, it can linger and become quite problematic.

I recommend you speak at length with your OB and pediatrician about this condition. It is a serious malady by itself but may also be indicative of a deeper form of depression. Enough said.

OPERATIONS

YOUR MISSION ORDERS

LEARN THE PROPER CARE and feeding of the NFU.

OPERATIONS

YOU THINK YOU'RE TIRED from the birth? Well, put on some coffee, Bubba. The fun's just starting.

Time to learn some nuts and bolts.

Let's rock 'n' roll.

THE NFU AT HOME

AFTER FORTY-EIGHT HOURS of extreme stress you arrive home, exhausted. If you're a smart man, you already have food in the freezer and a happy grandma standing by. You are tired but also "blissed out" and running on adrenaline. The NFU most likely is sleeping, and the FPP is sore and tired.

CRITICAL SURVIVAL TIP

Now may be a good time to share a glass of champagne with the FPP, if your doctor approves. She's spent the past ten months abstaining from booze, watching her diet, and focusing on launching a healthy NFU. Why not toast the new arrival? You both deserve it.

Go ahead, you earned it.

Once you get settled in, you suddenly realize: *there's not one doctor or nurse in here now.*

Don't panic, you'll do fine. There are a few things to be aware of right out of the gate.

PEE, POO, HURL, AND SNOT

IT MAKES *NO DIFFERENCE* how careful you are, you will encounter all four of these on a daily basis. Your hands and clothes will be fouled and you will smell things you thought existed only in a frat house bathroom. Get used to it, brother, it's part of the game. And trust me, after a couple of months, baby poo is about as annoying as engine grease; it's not fun to get under your nails, but it won't kill you, either. Just wash your hands and get on with it.

Be advised, your furniture will get wrecked as well. Infants will shower the couch with the above-mentioned bodily fluids and you will spill formula from time to time. And if the FPP is breast-feeding, expect spontaneous leakage. And don't get me started on toddlers, they're walking, talking grime machines.

For now, buy some slipcovers or just learn to live with it. After a couple of weeks of parenthood, the hurl stain on the couch will mean nothing.

CRITICAL SURVIVAL TIP

Babies can hurl from their noses with astonishing force. It will shock, amaze, and probably scare you at first, but be advised that it is most likely status quo. Ask your pediatrician about nose hurls for more in-depth information.

Babies aren't the only ones who can nose-hurl.
Marvin (above) is about to expel a giant cloud of warm gin.

HANDLING THE NFU

FROM THE VERY BEGINNING it's a good idea to get into the habit of washing your hands or using sanitizer every time you handle the NFU. Newbies are especially susceptible to germs, and as you've heard since grade school, germs are spread primarily by the human hand. Keep 'em clean, Ace.

Your pediatric nurse will show you how to hold your baby the proper way. After a couple of days you will find your own groove and use the grip that's most comfortable for you both. Just remember that her neck muscles are not developed, so you need to support her head for about the first four months. And FYI, there's actually a method called the "football hold."

Support the head, weird scary woman.

The following are miscellaneous notes related to those first few days at home:

- Babies cry, a lot. It may be because he's hungry or because he just peed with a newly circumcised tool. (This cry can be incredibly shrill. Imagine a porpoise being stuck with a hot fork.) Or he may just be testing his voice. Whatever the reason, try to relax. If there's a health issue, you will probably be able to tell instinctually. See "Health" for more on crying NFUs.
- Grandmas and friends will be dying to help. *Let them.* You will have tons of laundry, and the house will clutter up very quickly. Delegate chores and relax, for crying out loud.
- Doctors and nurses are just a phone call away if the fear starts to overwhelm you.
- You don't have to creep around the house in bare feet. In fact, studies show that babies sleep just fine with normal household noise. That is, unless your normal routine calls

for bagpipe solos or yodeling, in which case you may want to go out into the woods. *Way* out into the woods, thanks.

- You will have visitors, they will bring food, and it will be good. (Have hand sanitizer at the door.)
- You will be absolutely baffled and mystified as to how to proceed with life. Relax, watch the women, and jump right in. You will pick it up in no time.

REGARDING C-SECTION RECOVERY

IF YOUR FPP had a C-section, and chances are about 50-50 she did, there are a few important points to consider:

- She will be very sore for several weeks and may even be on bed rest for the first week at home, although most doctors encourage C-section moms to get on their feet immediately and engage in light activity.
- She will be unable to lift heavy objects for about six weeks, including baby furniture, groceries, etc.
- Stairs may be tough the first week or so.
- She may get very bored and possibly cranky because of the bed rest. Make certain she has books, magazines, a telephone, and TV nearby to kill the boredom.
- She will be unable to drive for the first two weeks, so work your schedule around trips to the doctor, grocery store, etc.

CRITICAL SURVIVAL TIP

The FPP will be bummed about the scar left by the C-section. The pain and the scar will subside; it's your job to tell her how great she looks while nature takes its course.

SLEEP — A MAJOR PARADIGM SHIFT

YOU'VE HEARD THE HORROR STORIES: Midnight feedings. Screeching baby, hours on end. Weeks with no sleep.

Are they true? Well, sort of.

Get used to this face; you will see it again.

When babies reach their fourth month or so, they start to find their own groove. Most sleep through the night.

But this book is all about the first few months, and during this time a baby keeps you awake, especially at feeding time, about every two to four hours.

Therefore, I pass on possibly the most important survival tip of all. Learn it, live it, love it:

CRITICAL SURVIVAL TIP

SLEEP WHEN BABY SLEEPS!!!

When the baby naps during the day or evening, you may have the urge to surf the Net or watch the game or even do some work at the home office. Trust me. You must sleep when the NFU sleeps because she will need food at 1:30 A.M. and you will wake up and probably stay that way. After a few days of this you feel fatigued, and it can affect your behavior at work or with the FPP. Sleep when you can.

But take heart: the kid eventually gets into a pattern, and you do, too.

THE SLEEPING NFU

EVEN SLEEP IS COMPLICATED when it comes to infants. You'd think they would just roll over and snore for eight hours like your aunt Melba, but no, they have issues in the crib as well.

Keep these points in mind:

* Babies make a wide variety of bizarre sleeping noises, ranging from grunts and wheezes to shrieks and whistles. These may be due to discomfort or simply the way they're wired. In any event, you intuitively learn to recognize what's important and filter out the rest.

* Make certain baby is sleeping on her back. This helps decrease the possibility of SIDS (sudden infant death syndrome), a scary but real possibility that you should discuss with your doctor.

* Babies like to be wrapped snugly in a warm blanket. Ask a nurse how to do this.

* Some infants really enjoy sleeping on Dad's chest. If yours does, just make sure his head is turned and breathing passages are clear.

- A baby monitor will save you plenty of trips up and down the stairs. A highly sensitive one-way radio, it picks up the slightest noise from the NFU. See the Glossary for details.

FEEDING

BREAST-FEED or formula?

This is something the FPP decides on her own. She may ask your opinion, but she makes the final call. It is a very personal decision for women, and your FPP has been researching the pros and cons for months now.

Regardless of which method is chosen, there are a number of issues you'll need to be aware of.

First, get familiar with the term *formula*. It's a specially manufactured liquid food used in place of breast milk for bottle-feeding the NFU. There are several types — some made from cow's milk, some from soy milk, and others from silverback gorilla milk. (Okay, I made that one up. Just testing to see if you're awake.) Some parents even manufacture their own formula to cut costs. More on formula choices later.

Even if you are breast-feeding, you may occasionally need to use formula when the FPP is unable to do her magic or when you are alone with the baby.

Let's take a look at the feeding methods.

BREAST-FEEDING

No matter how many times you witness it, you will squirm when you see the NFU having a snack on the fun bags that were your own personal recreation until about three months ago. But get used to it; this is how Junior eats, and he indulges often. (Don't be jealous, you'll get them back one day.) The breast-feeding process is actually quite fascinating, so try to put aside your urge to giggle like a teenage idiot and pay attention, you may learn something.

CRITICAL SURVIVAL TIP

Breast-feeding is a very personal issue for women. You may feel the urge to constantly crack jokes as a coping mechanism. Be advised, the FPP may be emotional and sensitive about the issue and you may suffer her wrath. This is bonding time for her and the NFU, and your jokes just aren't funny. Use tact.

Get familiar with these facts:

- Breast-feeding is good for the NFU. He gets extra antibodies and other valuable nutrients from Mom.
- Breast-feeding is not a solo effort. You will have the opportunity to feed the NFU from time to time, whether it's formula or breast milk that has been pumped by the FPP. I'll explain.
- Breast milk is easier than formula for the NFU to digest. It does not go well in Daddy's coffee, however.
- Breast-feeding can take a while, perhaps twenty minutes or longer.
- There are specialists called lactation consultants who can show your FPP how to work her gear. This could be a good investment because there's more to it than whipping them

out and squeezing. If problems arise, she may feel "inadequate" and need moral support as well as instruction.

- Your FPP will use a breast pump occasionally. This serves a number of purposes. Obviously, it's a good way to store milk for later. But it's also a way for her to relieve her breasts if they become engorged. (Yes, her teats may blow up like jack-o'-lanterns; no, you can't touch them.) The pumps come in many sizes and shapes, from simple manual ones to elaborate, electric double pumps. The process can be time-consuming and annoying, so try to pitch in around the house while she does her business.

- A "letdown" is a process by which the milk travels from some secret location in the FPP's chest down to the nipple, resulting in pain and possible leakage. Be advised, do *not* laugh when this happens.

CRITICAL SURVIVAL TIP

Get accustomed to the breast pump prior to the birth. Examine it, even take it apart, because when it's hooked up to your FPP and milk is shooting out like a dairy, you may lapse into shock or laugh so hard that a little pee comes out.

Breast-feeding may last only a week, or up to a few years, depending on the needs of the NFU and tolerance of the mother. In some cases children have been known to breast-feed well into grade-school years, but if you ask me, those are the kids who grow up to be clowns that bury their victims' bodies under the garage. Of course, that's my opinion and I know nothing about child psychology. Talk to your doctor about your long-term plans.

Weaning

The weaning process can take from a few days to a year or longer. It can be painful for the mom and distressful for you as you see her love cans deflate from head-size back to their prebaby mass. But, hey, don't complain. You loved them before she was pregnant and you will love them again.

FORMULA

There are many formula choices available, including those made from cow's milk and soy and those with special additives such as iron and vitamins. They all have pros and cons, and the main concerns for you as a dad are allergies and tolerance level, both of which should be discussed at length with your pediatrician.

For some odd reason, they all smell like dirty feet.

You can buy formula premade, which is pretty expensive, or you can buy the powder and make it yourself. While you save bucks doing this, be advised that it does take time and will give your FPP the "red ass" if she finds herself making formula every time.

Having said that, there are a few points to consider when preparing formula:

- Bottle sterilization. You need to boil the bottles, nipples, and lids every time you make formula, to make certain no microscopic critters find their way into the NFU's gut. Your dishwasher may be hot enough, but boiling is the sure bet.
- Sterilized water. Formula is made with sterilized (boiled) water. Buy yourself a cheap teapot to make the process easier.
- Shake well. The powder tends to coagulate and can clog up the nipples.

Bottle Operations

Not much to worry about here. Just be advised that bottles sometimes have weird internal-pressure issues that make the nipples collapse, causing the NFU to scream with frustration.

Caution: If you make formula ahead of time and store it in the fridge, do *not* microwave it before feeding the NFU. Even four seconds of radiation can kill the nutrients and make it dangerously hot. Place the bottle in a warm bowl of water instead.

Burping

Burp her often. NFUs suck down a ton of air (especially when very hungry), and burping prevents most major hurl episodes, which typically happen just after feeding or after she has been on her back for a few minutes.

There are a number of ways to execute the proper burp, which your pediatric nurse will be happy to demonstrate.

Gas Attacks

Babies have sensitive digestive systems and are especially susceptible to gas pains about feeding time. When an attack hits, they may kick, squirm, and cry until they fart, at which time they may start crying again from hunger. Yes, it is a vicious cycle.

One trick to help the NFU dislodge an air biscuit works like this:

Gently lay the little guy on a flat, soft surface (the crib or changing table will suffice). Then grab his ankles and *gently* pump his legs so that his knees move toward his chest. Do this several times and you may be rewarded with a large green cloud from his tail and a smile from his face.

Your doctor may also recommend over-the-counter anti-gas drops that purportedly decrease gas and its associated pains. After speaking with several fathers, I have determined that this product has about a 50 percent success rate. (No, this is not a scientific sample.)

Though to us gas is a minor annoyance (except after Cinco de Mayo), it causes major discomfort to your NFU. Be patient. BCF.

DIAPERS

ONE OF THE MOST FEARED aspects of father-hood is the diaper change.

The mechanics are baffling, and then there's the previously mentioned poo and pee.

CRITICAL SURVIVAL TIP

Get accustomed to carrying the diaper bag everywhere. In addition to diapers, wipes, and ointment, you will store food, toys, pacifiers, medicine, and other essentials in your lovely flower-covered lavender bag.

Relax. There's really nothing to it.

Here's the short story:

- Diapers are easy to change, especially the disposables. They are designed to fit a baby's butt, and the sticky tape seals things up tight.
- Newborns don't stink. The real funk kicks in at about two months.
- By the time they really start cranking out the fudge, you will have the process down to a science and know how to breathe strategically to avoid "poo gag."
- Baby wipes are key. You will go through thousands, literally.
- Little girls and little boys are wiped differently. Ask your nurse for a demo.
- You will learn about ointments and their place in the anti-chapping regimen. Basically, wet diapers cause rashes (red

ass), which in turn lead to incessant squawking. Ointments help prevent such misery.

- Diaper pails have come a long way. Many are relatively airtight and keep the funk inside. Some, such as the Diaper Genie, even encase the used diapers in a plastic sheath (just like sausages) for easy disposal.

CRITICAL SURVIVAL TIP

Little boys squirt you every chance they get. When removing their diapers, place a cloth or other soft object on their junk to avoid a hose-down. Be especially cautious if Junior is sporting wood; it means he's about to unload the bladder. Be prepared!

PLAYTIME

ONE OF THE HUGE UPSIDES to fatherhood is the recreation time.

For the first two months playtime is pretty limited, since the NFU is still in the alien phase. He has no real muscle control, and his eyesight is just a little better than that of a rainbow trout. In fact, his eyes may act independently (like an iguana's), which will definitely bug you out. But fear not: they sync up by the third month, and his vision begins to sharpen, at which time he starts to make eye contact with you and laugh when you make mouth noises.

This is also a good time to introduce toys and learning materials. Keep in mind that his neck is still weak and you still need to support his head, even though he's interacting with you.

Here are a few playtime suggestions for the post-alien-stage NFU:

- Hold him and dance to your favorite music.
- Lie back on the bed with the NFU at your side and read a book to him. Kids' books with bright illustrations are recommended, but he'll respond even if you're reading the *Wall Street Journal.* (He loves your voice, big guy.)
- Show him brightly colored infant toys, especially red, black, and white. His trout eyes can pick these colors up more easily than complex shades.

The bottom line is this: even though their feedback is limited, the NFUs love playing with Mom and Dad at this stage. Music, books, and toys are fine, but never underestimate the power of a well-timed duck noise or original story made up on the spot.

Before you know it, you'll be playing T-ball in the backyard, so enjoy the simple things while you can.

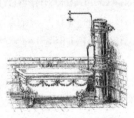

BATH TIME

SIMPLE RULE OF THUMB: bathe them when they stink, which is about every other day.

There are a number of products on the market that facilitate easy cleaning of the NFU, including a mesh ramplike object that sits in the bottom of the sink or adult tub.

Be advised of the following:

- Umbilical cords may be an issue. Ask your doctor how to proceed if part of the cord is still hanging on.
- *Never* leave an infant unattended in or near the water. But you already know that, right?
- NFUs are slippery when wet, Jack. Hold on tight.
- Be very aware of water temperature. What's warm to you could scald the NFU. Discuss ideal water temperature with your doctor.

Be advised: formula, drool, and yurp (hurl) gather in the neck region, and a heinous film grows. Be certain to dig down deep and avoid future foulness.

DRESSING THE NFU

WARNING! Defer all initial clothes issues to the FPP, or you will face her certain wrath!

You may make suggestions (quietly), but do not attempt to dress the NFU without the FPP's supervision. If the FPP chooses an outfit in advance and leaves the room, you may then proceed to dress the NFU.

You will have plenty of time to suggest outfits as Junior gets older; for now, let her call the shots.

You have been warned.

SLINGS, SWINGS, AND BOUNCIES

BY NOW, you've probably been educated about the gear piled up in your game room and how most of it operates. Hopefully, the baby shower hooked you up hard and you still have a little golf-ball money in your sock drawer.

Or maybe not.

The Glossary goes into detail about gear and confusing terms, but there are a few items I highly recommend right out of the escape hatch:

- The sling is a remarkable over-the-shoulder pouch that replicates the womb. It's a bit difficult to operate at first, but fortunately, the makers offer a video that takes you through the steps. Babies love the comforting nature of the device, and it's great for quieting agitated NFUs.

- You're already familiar with car seats, but what you may not know is that they make a great "portable crib" you can carry around the house. For instance, say you need to work in the basement but can't leave the NFU alone in his crib. Strap him into his car seat and rock 'n' roll. Be certain to keep the rats away.

- Bouncy chairs rule. They're more appropriate for babies with neck control, so you may have to wait a couple of months, but they're definitely worth it.

- Swings are great for calming the NFU in mid-meltdown. Certain models have battery-operated motors with speed control that will save your life from time to time. Just strap the baby in and let 'er rip. Keep it on the lowest setting for now, or feel the hurl.

HEALTH

YOUR MISSION ORDERS

LEARN PROPER HEALTH CARE and physical maintenance of the NFU.

HEALTH

TIPS RELATED TO HEALTH-CARE issues follow. Again, these are *not* medical recommendations but, rather, general tips and guidelines that may help you deal with a very stressful evolution.

If you have any questions, concerns, or anxieties about health issues, call your doctor. (Yes, my lawyer likes this phrase.)

CRITICAL SURVIVAL TIP

You can take courses in infant CPR and first aid. Check with your local hospital, American Red Cross, or YMCA for details.

One of the harsh realities of parenthood is illness and injury. Nothing is worse than seeing your little one sick or hurt.

CRITICAL SURVIVAL TIP

When your child is sick or injured, you feel absolutely helpless and may even panic, a natural, innate reaction that is especially intense the first few times it happens. We can't control these events, and as men and warriors, it rips our heart out. Keep a cool head and follow your doctor's instructions and chances are that things will be fine. Panic is no good for anyone. Pediatricians deal with stressed-out parents every day. Trust them; your NFU is in good hands.

You have prepared well and have your pediatrician's number on speed dial. You should also have the number posted by every telephone, at home and work, just in case. And also give the number to grandparents as a safety net.

CRYING, WAILING, AND MOANING

UNTIL YOU HAVE A CHILD of your own, a crying baby sounds like fingernails on a chalkboard. Or cats fighting. Or a smoke detector. But when those sounds are coming from your NFU, they inspire a whole new set of emotions: fear, worry, annoyance, and, yes, even joy.

A baby's cries are obviously his way of communicating, and at this age his wants and needs are very simple: food, clean diaper, companionship, and relief from pain.

If he is hungry, he cries. If he has a funky diaper, he may wail — and so might you. If you're in the other room and he's alone in the crib, he may squawk to get your attention. And if he's sick, he may cry endlessly and drive you mad. But this is what babies do, and in very short order you will be able to distinguish one cry from another.

CRITICAL SURVIVAL TIP

Some babies suffer from *colic*, a condition indicated by non-stop bouts of wailing that start for no apparent reason. There is no firm definition of the condition (it's not a disease), but experts speculate that it may be caused by excessive gas (go on, admit it, it makes you piss and moan, too), food allergies, or intolerance and stress around the house (yes, they can sense when you are freaked out). If your NFU's crying patterns change dramatically or become more intense, be sure to mention it to your doctor.

SOOTHING THE HOWLING BEAST

THERE ARE A NUMBER of tried-and-true ways to chill out the NFU, even one who is colicky:

- holding him and singing or humming softly
- creating motion — rocking chairs, strollers, even carrying him around in a car seat might work
- giving him a pacifier (You will see this again.)
- massaging his back lightly
- wrapping him in a cocoon (Ask the nurse to show you how. It works!)
- giving him a warm bath (but may also piss him off)
- carrying him in a sling

There are many other strategies that work, and you'll find one that works best for you. *Hint:* Ask one of the grandmothers what worked for her.

> **CRITICAL SURVIVAL TIP**
> Pacifiers are absolute miracles of nature. They're a personal choice and should be cleared with your doctor, but believe me, these little three-dollar pieces of plastic can turn a raging NFU into a lamb in seconds. See the Glossary for details.

FEVERS

Very few babies make it through their first few months without a fever. It makes them cranky, and quite frankly it will scare the hell out of you the first time it happens. There are several indicators of fever:

- His forehead seems unusually warm when you kiss it.
- He's cranky or lethargic.
- A rectal (ouch) thermometer reads above 100 degrees.
- He has convulsions.

If you do suspect fever, call your doctor. He or she will most likely talk you through the cool-down process. This may include

- giving the NFU infant Tylenol
- applying a cool compress
- giving a cool bath

The doctor will need to know the baby's specific temperature, so familiarize yourself with the various types of thermometers on the market.

CRITICAL SURVIVAL TIP

Your pharmacist can make suggestions as to which type of thermometer is age-appropriate for the NFU. It will most likely be a rectal variety but may also be a fancy type that is used in the ear. Prices vary greatly, so shop around.

If the fever seems high or if the cooling methods fail to bring down the baby's temperature, the doctor may ask to see her, to play it safe. Remember: your doctor has seen nearly every situation imaginable, so don't panic and don't scream at the FPP or kick the cat. Wrap up your NFU to prevent chills and take her to the doctor's office as directed. And BCF.

EARACHES

FOR SOME REASON this seems to be another trouble spot for babies. Infections take hold and, man, will you know about it. Not only will the NFU scream like a banshee, he will tug or bat at his ears. Sometimes you may even see discharge. In many cases fever accompanies an earache. If you suspect this is the problem, go ahead and schedule an appointment with the doctor; it's not something you can fix at home.

RASHES

MOST BABIES SUFFER diaper rash (aka "chapped ass") at some point, and there are over-the-counter remedies to soothe her butt. However, some rashes can be an indication of something more serious, such as allergies, so keep a vigilant watch over any rashes that appear in weird places or hang around for more than a day or two. A quick call to the doctor will ease your mind in most cases.

There are a number of ways to prevent rashes (especially the diaper variety):

* Keep the butt dry after bathing. Allow Junior's arse to dry off, then powder it before throwing on the diaper.
* Certain clothing may irritate your NFU's skin. Keep a close watch. And whatever you do, don't dress him in burlap. Trust me, it's ugly.
* Change diapers often. Wet diapers are usually the main cause of diaper rash.

EMERGENCY ROOMS

I HATE TO BREAK this to you, but according to statistics, you will most likely visit the emergency room several times during your child's early years. Granted, most visits will be after the NFU starts walking (and falling), but you may need to visit the hospital in the first few months, especially for persistent fevers or related maladies. Talk to your pediatrician to determine what illnesses justify a visit to the ER.

And, of course, there may be simple household accidents that necessitate a visit to the ER.

So here's the drill:

The emergency room should have been called "wait for two damn hours with other hurt people room."

Be prepared to encounter other injured or sick people who are as freaked out as you are, even in the middle of the night.

And be prepared to wait for hours, unless it's a life-or-death situation.

I've spoken to dozens of parents, and the unanimous consensus about emergency rooms is: *They only rush to get your insurance card.*

(Settle down, Doc. It's just a joke.)

Most hospitals are very good at performing triage and classifying priorities. This means that when you arrive at the ER, a nurse will examine the NFU immediately and determine whether the situation is critical or whether it can wait until the wino with the screwdriver in his neck is attended to first.

In your mind, your NFU is more important than everyone else there and you will fight the primitive urge to scream at the nurses for moving too slowly.

BCF.

If they think your baby is in danger, they will take him right away.

The following is a typical scenario:

Let's assume it's midnight and your NFU has a persistent fever but is in no immediate danger; he's breathing fine but is fussy. You called your pediatrician and he counseled you to go to the ER, to play it safe.

CRITICAL SURVIVAL TIP

You can call the hospital from your cell phone while in transit to the emergency room. This may not speed up the process, but it doesn't hurt to inform them that you're bringing in a sick infant.

You arrive at the hospital and park near the ER door; parking is easier to find at night.

Rather than carrying the baby in your arms, you take him in the car seat so that he has a place to sleep while you wait and wait.

You enter the ER, find the reception desk, and check in. If it's a critical emergency (in this case, it's not), they have a nurse triage the NFU right away. Otherwise, they take your billing information and insurance card and enter you into the system. You are then asked to take a seat in the waiting area. (Try to avoid the aforementioned wino.)

After a few minutes, the nurse (or similar health-care professional) calls your name and you go back for triage, which takes a couple of minutes and basically involves vital signs and a Q&A session about the baby's history and recent health.

Once the nurse has a thumbnail sketch of the NFU's situation, he sends you back to the waiting area and then passes the record on to the duty doctor.

This is when the fun starts. Grab a magazine and find a comfortable seat; it may be a while. Be sure to keep the NFU comfortable and call any concerned relatives and let them know that everything is cool.

EDUCATE THYSELF

THROUGHOUT THE BOOK I've hammered home the importance of doctors' advice. This is because health issues are the most stressful events you encounter as a parent. Even money stresses pale in comparison to a sick baby, especially when your little girl cries nonstop through the night and you can't comfort her despite your best efforts.

One way to ease the stress is to research infant-related health issues and keep solid, proven reference materials on hand. While these *do not* take the place of your physician's advice, they can provide insight to the biomechanics of the NFU and help you understand what's going on when he has an ear infection, cold, or other malady.

You can pick these up online or at your local book-store:

- *Caring for Your Baby and Young Child*, by the American Academy of Pediatrics
- *Baby Basics: A Guide for New Parents*, by Anne K. Blocker, RD
- *The Baby Book: Everything You Need to Know About Your Baby From Birth to Age Two* (revised and updated edition), by William Sears, MD, and Martha Sears, RN

You can also find great information online. Just go with caution, lad. You know better than to trust everything you read, especially on the Internet. These sites seem to have consistently reliable information:

- WebMD.com
- BabyCenter.com
- Babies.com

Knowledge is power. Just make sure you're filling your head with reliable facts and not some wacko speculation.

ANCILLARY DUTIES

YOUR MISSION ORDERS

RE-ESTABLISH AND MAINTAIN a personal life outside of the parenthood box.

ANCILLARY DUTIES

THERE'S MORE TO RAISING babies than just raising babies. You have lives, too. Don't forget to take care of your business.

DATING THE FPP

THIS MAY SEEM AN ODD thing to suggest, but think about it: for nine months you've both been completely consumed with the pregnancy. Now that the NFU is here, your household roles have experienced a major paradigm shift: you are Dad, she is Mom.

But you're both still people and need to keep that in mind, or you could drift apart. So how do you reconnect with the FPP? Simple. Start dating again.

You need a grandma or other child-care provider to sit with the NFU. Grandmas are the preferred choice, as you trust them implicitly and can therefore actually enjoy your date.

CRITICAL SURVIVAL TIP

The first time you leave the NFU with someone other than the FPP, you will be a nervous wreck. It's a good idea to have Grandma act as the first babysitter so that you'll be able to relax and enjoy the company of your FPP. Be advised, all conversations will be about the NFU anyway.

If you are breast-feeding, then either plan your date around feedings or leave a bottle for Grandma.

Keep your cell phone charged and ready. You will worry constantly about your NFU and will probably call six or ten times. This is natural and expected. Just keep in mind that the NFU will probably not miss you for a couple of hours, unless he gets hungry or poops, in which case Grandma knows what to do. Relax, pal, and have a good time.

SEX AND THE GREAT BOOB IRONY

SEEMS LIKE FOREVER, doesn't it? Don't worry, it happens to all of us. From about month seven of the pregnancy until two months after the birth, sex is a faded memory, unless you sneak off to the computer room after midnight and punch up your favorite "adult site" and have some quality me time. (This I don't want to know about.) But I can tell you this: when she was going through the birth and screamed,

"You're never touching me again, you bastard!"

she probably didn't mean it. You will live again, and it will be good.

So when do the games begin again? Typically about six weeks after the birth the FPP goes in for an equipment checkup. If she gets the okay from the doc, she may be ready for a little tentative fun. But don't be discouraged if she's not ready to have a gymnastics meet with you; she's still sore down there, and nothing kills a romantic meeting like a shooting pain in the naughty bits. (Imagine trying to get freaky with a bee stinging your balls.)

Have patience with her and before you know it, you'll be back to your normal sweaty selves.

THE GREAT BOOB IRONY

You've seen the FPP's breasts swell throughout the pregnancy and, man, do they look good. But you won't be able to have any fun with these new supersize toys unless, of course, you don't mind a face full of she-milk every time you get within a foot of the muzzles.

So you abstain until the breast-feeding evolution is secured and then one day the FPP finally gives you permission to play again and — *surprise!* — they've returned to their prepregnancy state.

Isn't it ironic?

BIRTH CONTROL?

THAT'S RIGHT, time to start counting your bullets. Shortly after birth the FPP may *technically* be ready to conceive again (psychologically is a different matter), and are you really ready for the roller coaster this soon?

Talk it over with her, and decide on a method. You know the drill.

STRESS RELIEF

YOUR NFU WILL STRESS YOU OUT. Believe it. And combined with professional demands, marital issues, sleep deprivation, traffic, a vomiting cat, and world events, the stress compounds. It is crucial that you blow off steam; otherwise, you may start kicking inanimate objects or experience shooting pains up your left arm (and you know what's next!). It is imperative that you find an hour or two for yourself a few times per week to get some exercise and clear your head. Make it physical and do it outside of the home. You love your NFU intensely, but time alone is absolutely critical. And make time for your FPP to train as well; her stress levels are also elevated, and she wants to "get her body back."

If you enjoy exercising with the FPP, you can:

- play tennis
- hike
- play golf
- mountain bike
- swim

These activities are fun and promote good health. Does this sound like a government pamphlet, or what? Let's continue with more fun bullet points!

EXERCISE TIPS

- Elevate your pulse rate at least thirty minutes a day, three or four times a week. Try kickboxing, cycling, swimming, or even chopping wood. Increased aerobic activity not only relieves stress but also facilitates weight loss. And you know you put on an extra ten just as she did, so hit the gym, doughnut boy.

- Always stretch before and after, especially if you're sleep-deprived. This eases some of the pain in your back.

- Most experts agree that weight training has the most overall benefit, if done rigorously and consistently, even three times a week. You will need added strength when attempting to give your toddler cough medicine a year from now, so train hard now.

- Wear headphones and listen to your favorite tunes. It gives you some time in your own head without other family members squawking relentlessly in your ear.

- If you wear a top hat and tails to the gym, you may get thrashed mercilessly.

BEWARE . . .

THERE ARE SEVERAL inherent problems that make stress relief difficult. The most obvious is time management. Your schedule may be full, but you must make the time. A solid workout can kill two birds (stress relief and weight loss) with one stone, and you'll feel great afterward. *But you must make the time.* Your family and your heart will thank you.

Another problem can be *choice* of stress relief. For example, prior to the NFU, you played golf twice a week. If you even mention golf to your FPP during the first three months of parenthood, be certain to wear a helmet and flak jacket. Your suggestion will fall on unsympathetic ears and may ignite a raging hissy fit, to say the least. It is recommended that you find something in the two-hour range until the NFU is a bit older.

"Back off, tool! I've got a newborn at home!"

The bottom line is this: your family loves you and needs you to be clearheaded and calm around the house. So BCF. Stress can wear you down and make you miserable. Take care of yourself.

CRITICAL SURVIVAL TIP

Parenthood is a major head trip, and your emotions will vac-
illate wildly. Stress compounds this effect, and you will have
the urge to scream at everyone around you, including the
NFU, especially when she's kept you up all night, crying for
no apparent reason. And you will hate yourself a split second later. To avoid this scenario, work out a plan with your
FPP that allows you to bail immediately when you start feel-
ing steam shoot from your ears. Go for a drive, take a walk,
shoot some hoops . . . the stress will pass.

SURVIVING THE JOB

SO YOUR FAMILY is squared away and it's back to
the office. What's the big deal? Well, there are several.

TIME MANAGEMENT

- You need time off for visits to the pediatrician.
- You need more time in the mornings to help the FPP "get
  the day going."
- If the FPP has a career (most do), you need to juggle your
  schedule to accommodate her needs.
- Schedule an extra hour a few times a week for a workout.
  Sounds simple, but just try it.
- You will make dozens of extra stops at the pharmacy or gro-
  cery store for diapers. Allow time.

GUILT AND EMOTIONS

YOU WILL MISS THE NFU. At first, time back at the office seems like a relief, but then a huge wave of emotion hits you, distracting you and possibly even causing your work to suffer. (So what? It's your first kid. Work can just damn well wait.)

It's okay to feel guilt for not being home with the baby.

THE HORROR THAT
IS THE HOME OFFICE

IF YOU WORK AT HOME, you have a whole different set of issues to deal with now. Under normal conditions, it's a great setup; you work in your sweats and commute fifteen feet from your recliner to your desk.

Big changes now, mate.

Just imagine: You're on the phone, troubleshooting for a big client in New York when in the background the NFU melts down, the overnight delivery guy rings the doorbell, and the FPP signals, "Honey, I need your help!" all at the same time.

You try to play it off, but the client politely signs off with a "Hey, take care of your situation, we can talk later," dreaded words for the self-employed warrior.

The following are a few tips to keep you on track at the home office:

- Set aside definite "work hours" and stick to them. Try to plan around times that the NFU may need you, such as feedings or diaper changes.

- Move your office to a quiet room, close the door, and put up a DO NOT DISTURB sign. This may frost the FPP but, hey, you gotta pay the bills, right?
- Play a small radio in the background to drown out noise from the other rooms in the house.

CRITICAL SURVIVAL TIP

Set aside specific "daddy hours" during the day and break away completely from the office (no phones, no e-mail) and play with the family. Dinnertime is especially good, since your clients are probably wrapping up the day as well. You can always go back to the desk when the NFU goes to bed.

It is possible to run a business from home with an NFU in the next room, but be advised that it takes discipline and focus and that the NFU knows you only as Daddy, not the great corporate raider in the next room.

CHILDCARE

UNFORTUNATELY, Grandma isn't always going to be around to sit with Junior, and you need to start looking for an alternative caregiver.

I'm warning you now. This will be a thorny issue, and the fur may fly when it comes to choosing a sitter, especially the first time you leave the NFU with someone other than a grandmother. The FPP may be a bit more at ease with caregivers, but you will have a primitive reaction that may daze and confuse you.

Hey, we've all seen the hidden-camera videos, right?

As men, we are slaves to millions of years of evolution and still believe deep inside that a jackal could burst through our door any second and run off with our progeny. So how in hell are we supposed to trust a fourteen-year-old neighborhood girl to protect the heir to our empire?

Sounds extreme, but you can bet your softball spikes (you won't need them anyway) that you'll distrust every babysitter who bops through the door, even the cute one from across the street who just got home from college.

Take heart, brother. "Caregiver abuse" is a pretty rare phenomenon, and unless you live on the Serengeti, jackal attacks are virtually nonexistent, so you can put your can of Whup-ass back on the shelf and relax.

Childcare is an inevitable part of parenthood, and you're not the first dad to stress the issue. By conducting interviews and even background checks, you can find a competent, caring caregiver who will protect your legacy as her own and may even kick the jackal's teeth in, should it find its way through the doggy door. And the college girl? She may be perfectly well suited for the job, especially if she has younger brothers or sisters or is studying education and needs the money. It's worth an interview.

"Hee-hee. I found dirty magazines in the closet!"

CRITICAL SURVIVAL TIP

Ask your friends, coworkers, or pediatrician for caregiver referrals. Be advised: some parents are very protective of their babysitters and are hesitant to share the information and may give you the stink eye in lieu of a phone number. You may have to grease them to get the digits.

Let's look at the different options.

NANNIES, SITTERS, AU PAIRS, OH MY!

OH, STOP IT.

All those stories you hear from your buddies are a crock, and if they are shagging the sitter, they should be poleaxed and jailed.

Now wipe off the grin so we can get started, eh?

CRITICAL SURVIVAL TIP

Regardless of what child-care method you choose, be diligent about checking references. And in the case of commercial day-care facilities, be sure that they are in compliance with all state licensing requirements.

THE TWO BASIC CATEGORIES

BASICALLY, you have two options right out of the gate: out-of-home (or remote) and in-home.

OUT-OF-HOME/REMOTE
There are a number of options in this category, including:

- private caregivers
- day-care centers
- church nurseries
- preschools

If you follow the national average, you will probably choose a private caregiver or day-care center. Let's deconstruct a few.

Private Caregiver
This is typically a parent who takes a small group of kids (in addition to her own) into her home and charges a reasonable hourly rate. She should have a state license in order to do this and will probably ask you to sign some sort of contract or agreement that lays out her responsibilities and expectations, including meals, clothing changes, naps, etc. She should also be willing to

provide a list of references upon request, and you should speak with other parents before making a decision.

There are pros and cons to working with a private caregiver.

PROS

- Groups are small, and your kid gets more attention and bonds with the caregiver.
- Fewer kids means friendships form faster.
- The caregiver may be willing to take the NFU overnight, on weekends, or during emergencies.
- It's cheaper than commercial day-care centers.
- The setting is more like home and less like school, which is key for very young kids.

CONS

- They may lack formal structure.
- Your schedule can be thrown off if the caregiver gets sick or takes an unexpected day off.
- Caregivers often work alone and get stressed out.
- Germs are rampant. (You will see this again.)
- Safety and cleanliness requirements may not be as strict as at commercial facilities.

Day-Care Centers

Commercial day-care centers can be found everywhere; it seems that even the smallest towns have one or two facilities and that they're always busy. (Baby making is apparently a universal sport.) They may be part of a national franchise or simply run by a sole operator or family. They're located in churches, converted schools, office parks, and their own stand-alone buildings. They're typically regulated by the state in which they operate and are subject to strict licensing, sanitary, and operational rules. They are often more expensive than private caregivers and in some cases can be very difficult to crack. Day-care centers with good reputations may very well have a waiting list of a year or longer.

PROS

- They tend to be structured and instill stability.
- The staff are usually properly trained and in some cases may hold education degrees.
- Centers have kids from varied ethnic, religious, and cultural backgrounds.
- Centers are subject to strict state regulation.
- There may be an educational element, even for the very young children.
- You will probably be invited in for conferences to discuss the NFU's development and progress.

CONS

- The expense can be greater than other forms of childcare.
- A contract is probably required, and you are charged even when the NFU stays home for a week.
- There is less one-on-one instruction.
- With bigger classes, there is more potential for the NFU to find trouble, which he will once he starts walking.

- Hours are less flexible.
- Germs are rampant here, too.

IN-HOME CARE

Just what it sounds like. You have someone come to your house and take care of baby while you hunt and gather. It can be a grandmother, babysitter, nanny, au pair, or family friend. She may cook and clean or even snoop through the top drawer in your bedroom dresser, the one with the old cigar, class ring, and loose change.

NANNIES are pros, women (and occasionally men, called "mannies") with special training who are hired specifically to care for your child. They may have CPR and first aid training as well as advanced nutritional and educational skills. They may live in your home or commute, depending on your budget and their needs. They can be found through referrals or by contacting an agency that screens the candidates on your behalf. And, of course, there's an agency fee, but it's better than running an ad in the paper and having two dozen toothless, jabbering sociopaths call to offer their "services." You wouldn't let a stranger from the classifieds drive your car around the block. Would you really trust one to keep the NFU for hours at a time, unsupervised? Enough said. Nannies' fees are negotiable and should be discussed right out of the gate. Be certain to discuss transportation, meal, and overtime expenses.

AU PAIRS are typically young women from foreign countries who exchange fifty hours per week of child-care services for travel expenses, room and board, and

maybe a small weekly stipend. (I told you to stop grin-
ning like a hyena.) They may have advanced training in
the infant maintenance arts, but probably not. They're
most likely eighteen to twenty-five years old and looking for a way to get to the States for a little sightseeing
and R and R. Nothing wrong with that in theory, except
that you as a parent really need someone who has her
head in the game when it comes to the NFU. They may
stay for a few months or contract for a year or longer.
Be advised, however, over the long term, you may run
into some tricky immigration and employment issues.
Au pairs can be found through agencies as well, and
they usually do a very good job at screening out the
flakes. Just be certain to ask tough questions when you
interview her:

- If my child is having a bad day and cries a great deal, will
  you come unglued and shake him like a three-dollar Sponge
  Bob doll, or react in a rational, adult manner?
- Do you plan to drink my liquor and fill the bottle back up
  with water so I won't notice?
- Can you handle emergencies, or will you run from the house
  screaming as if your ass were on fire?
- Will you treat my home like a bordello, or will you shag
  American boys on your own time, at a location other than
  my basement floor?
- Will you stay the hell out of my cigar drawer?

There are certainly au pairs out there who are con-
summate experts who behave with the utmost dedica-
tion, skill, and professionalism. (I don't need any hate

mail from au pair agencies, so don't bother.) However, this father has seen how the au pair system can fly off the tracks when a young woman from a Third World nation is turned loose to sample the riches of American suburbia. Go with caution, brother.

Pros and cons associated with in-home childcare follow.

PROS

- The NFU gets to stay at home, meaning fewer germs and a more familiar environment.
- You have control over whom you hire and ultimately who enters your home.
- No commute to/from a child-care facility.
- The NFU's schedule stays consistent.
- The caregiver plays by your rules.
- Baby gets individual attention.
- The caregiver may be willing to take care of household chores and cook and may even wash your car and dig the mud out of your golf clubs. But don't push it, Jack; this is about the kid.

CONS

- There are no playmates for the NFU.
- The caregiver is your employee, and you have to deal with issues such as her taxes, benefits, etc.
- It can be more expensive than remote childcare, and you also have to factor in transportation, meals, etc.
- You may need liability insurance to cover her.

- If the caregiver gets sick, you're screwed.
- You'll give up some privacy.
- The NFU may form an especially tight bond with the caregiver, which may frost you and the FPP or cause a sense of jealousy.

BABYSITTERS

THIS IS AN EASY ONE. It's a person who watches over your NFU for a short period of time while you and the FPP go out to dinner to get away from the NFU but end up talking about him the whole time anyway.

Typically, one pictures a young neighborhood girl when thinking of a sitter, but it could be a friend from work, a relative, or another new parent from your childbirth-education class.

Here are a few guidelines related to sitters:

- Obviously, if you hire a teenager from the neighborhood, be certain she knows what to do in an emergency.
- Leave your cell number as well as the number of a close relative and the pediatrician.
- Give special instructions regarding food, changing diapers, etc.
- Let her know if the NFU has any special needs at bedtime, i.e., passy, music, etc.
- Leave snacks for her.
- Have her show up a half hour early so the NFU can acclimate to her voice, etc.
- Tip well if she does a good job.

CRITICAL SURVIVAL TIP

Some child-care expenses can be deducted from your taxes. For God's sake, man, hire an accountant and get some money back!

For further information about childcare, check out *Baby Basics* by Anne K. Blocker.

CHILDPROOFING

AS YOU HAVE now discovered, the scope of this book ranges from late pregnancy to about six months. You won't need to worry about childproofing until nine months or so, when Junior starts pulling himself across the floor toward the stairs.

Be advised, however, you need to start planning now for a whole new household standard operating procedure. Electrical outlets get plugged, staircases gated, and sharp objects placed out of reach.

Most babyproofing gear is relatively inexpensive, but it is necessary. Start saving now.

"Coming, dear!"

GLOSSARY

YOUR MISSION ORDERS

LEARN, UNDERSTAND, AND ABSORB definitions of critical gear, equipment, and events relative to the parenting objective.

GLOSSARY

THE FOLLOWING LIST includes terms, objects, and gear you will encounter over the next few months. They may seem like Mandarin Chinese now, but by month six they will be part of your daily vocabulary.

Note: Several of these, especially the babyproofing items, apply to kids in the one-year range. For example, you won't need toilet seat locks until the NFU is about a year old. Be advised: time rockets by and it's smart to plan ahead.

CRITICAL SURVIVAL TIP

You should research all gear before buying, to ensure it complies with federal safety standards. One great resource is *Consumer Reports: Guide to Baby Products*, available at bookstores, online, or at the library. In addition to detailed specifications about every imaginable product on the market, the book lists recently recalled products that may pose a danger to your NFU.

A&D OINTMENT Translucent baby-lube-in-a-tube. A greasy unguent roughly the color of old chicken broth and souped up with vitamins A and D (thus the name, Watson), A&D ointment is used primarily to treat diaper rash. (See "Diaper Rash.") It works kind of like Turtle Wax on a Porsche, keeping damaging moisture away from the tender surface of the NFU's nether regions.

CRITICAL SURVIVAL TIP

A&D ointment comes in a tube very similar to those used by Crest, Colgate, and other toothpaste companies. Do *not*, in a bleary-eyed morning moment after an attack of NPSD (new parent sleep disorder), make the mistake of grabbing the baby lube in lieu of the Crest. It tastes hideous and is nearly impossible to clean off of your toothbrush. Not that I would know, or anything.

AFTERBIRTH Obsolete placenta, expelled from the uterus following the birth of the NFU. In some mammalian societies, the FPP consumes the nutrient-laden organ to provide strength during the postpartum period. (You'll never eat liver again.)

AU PAIR No, it's not French for "hot young babysitter." An au pair is typically a full-time child-care professional from a foreign country who works in exchange for room and board and a small stipend. You find them through agencies, and contracts typically run for one year and are renewable depending on immigration guidelines, work permits, etc. You should be able to interview her before hiring, and if you accept her as an employee, you will pay for her ticket to and from her home country.

CRITICAL SURVIVAL TIP

If you hire a young woman to be your au pair, expect her to act like a young woman, especially in her off-duty hours. She is, after all, in a new, exciting country. She will find the single guys in your neighborhood, or they will find her. Be certain to clarify your policies as to visitors, hours, etc., before signing a contract. And for God's sake, don't even think about it!

BABY BJORN A specially made pouch for the NFU. Baby can face the parent or out toward the world.

BABY FOOD In addition to the common jar food such as Gerber's, this term also encompasses formula, cereal, and breast milk. When the FPP tells you to "pack the baby food," make certain you have her specify the exact type; otherwise, you will pay dearly for the mistake ten minutes into the road trip.

BABY POWDER There are different types of powder for different skin types, health conditions, etc. It is usually applied all over the body but especially in the moist regions. (Do the math.) Your pediatrician and FPP will instruct you as to the proper brand. Be advised that if your store does not carry this specific brand, drive and drive some more until you find it. Trust me.

BABYPROOFING Any alteration in a room aimed at protecting the NFU from harm, e.g., plug covers for electrical outlets, child-resistant cabinet latches, and tennis ball halves over sharp corners.

BABY SEAT A portable molded-plastic, padded seat with a carrying handle that can be swung around the back to double as a seat prop. Some models are curved to allow gentle rocking. When the NFU reaches the developmental stage at which he or she can generate a pendulum motion, take care where you place the baby seat, lest the NFU "rock 'n' roll" right off the table.

BABY SHOWER Not a cleansing device. The baby shower is an FPP-to-be celebratory ritual, held in anticipation of the arrival of the NFU. Think of shower as in *rain*, as in "raining gifts." The female support network of the FPP-to-be gathers together to provide layette items and other NFU accessories and gear. Lady food, such as finger sandwiches, little cakes, and exotic salads, is usually served. The loot is ceremoniously unwrapped by the FPP, and the room erupts in dolphinlike shrieks of approval. Be advised, you are to remain on the premises, invisible but available to haul oversize gift items.

BABY WIPES Disposable, premoistened towelettes for sanitizing the NFU's diaper zone as well as cleaning up hurl. In fact, they're also great for cleaning up spilled food, splattered formula, and just about any other baby-related mess. *Note:* You can buy the house brand at most major grocery stores and save big bucks.

BACK LABOR The FPP may feel the brunt of the uterine bludgeoning, aka contractions from hell, in her back muscles. Counterpressure with tennis balls or rolling pins (not kidding, Ace) sometimes helps. If you use a rolling pin, be aware of the possibility that in a pain-prompted fugue state, the FPP may seize and wield it. Keep your wits about you.

BALMEX (DESITIN, ZINC OXIDE) Opaque pasty baby-lube-in-a-tube. Another diaper-rash emollient substance, whitish due to the addition of zinc oxide, so double the warning regarding toothpaste errors.

BASSINET A basket for the NFU. Can be port-able or stationary with legs.

BATHTUB There are several very clever tubs for your NFU, who in the first several months is squirmy and slick. These tubs make bathing safe and reasonably simple. *Under no circumstances* should you bathe the NFU in a full-size tub without the FPP's permission. Doing so could result in an axe kick in the back from the FPP.

BED PROPPERS A double-sided cloth wedge that holds the squirmy NFU.

BEDSIDE SLEEPER A small, portable crib-like apparatus that allows the NFU to safely sleep in the bed with parents.

BIB Slop catcher. False shirtfronts made of soft plastic or fabric, sometimes with moisture-resistant backing, bibs are designed to protect the NFU's garments from feeding fallout. They come in a variety of styles and sizes, from micro-human to industrial-strength.

BINKY See "Pacifier."

BOOSTER SEAT A seat constructed to bring the NFU up to table level. Some portable booster seats are legless, having clamps for direct table attachment.

BOOTIES No, not those booties. The little sock-like shoes that keep the NFU's feet warm.

BOUNCY CHAIR A clever cloth seat fitted to a wire frame that allows the NFU to sit upright and bounce at will.

BREAST PUMP Suction device for downloading breast milk from mammary glands. Think dairy farm. Think mechanical milker. There you have it. (Do not share this line of thinking with the FPP, as she may take offense at the bovine analogy.) Can be manual or electronic. Can have single- or double-pumping capacity. (It's best not to overthink this.) May cause spontaneous laughter on your part. BCF.

BURPING A rubbing or gentle patting action that facilitates a belch from a recently fed NFU. May prevent hurls and yurps.

CARRIAGE Sleeping module on wheels. Can be as simple as a rickshaw or as elaborate as an Airstream.

CAR SEAT Baby bucket seats designed for optimum protection during automobile travel. Car seats are regulated by law and must conform to safety standards. Proper installation of the seat in the vehicle according to manufacturer's instructions is essential. Proper installation of the NFU in the car seat according to manufacturer's instructions is also essential. (See Parents.com website for consumer safety information on car seats.)

CEREAL No, not Count Chocula. The NFU's first solid food consisting of finely milled or flaked grain, cereal can be purchased premixed or dried. If dried, it needs wet stuff added to it — water, formula, juice, or even, yes, breast milk. Rice cereal, as the least allergenic, is the starter cereal. After the NFU passes the six-month mark, oat, barley, or wheat can be added to the menu.

CHANGING TABLE Practically speaking, any flat surface on which the NFU can be laid out for the process of de- and re-diapering. As a nursery furnishing, a changing table can be strictly utilitarian, a table with a flat pad on top and few shelves underneath, or a functionally stylish "changing station," designed for ease of one-handed retrieval of changing supplies. (The other hand should always be on the NFU, to prevent roll-offs.)

CRADLE Traditional sleeping module on rockers. Rocks the NFU to sleep.

CRIB Elevated stationary sleeping module, with sides, often bars, to prevent the NFU's escape. Wide range of styles and quality. Often some assembly is required. (Get used to this, and always keep a set of Allen wrenches and a Phillips screwdriver handy.) Be advised, some cribs have been subject to recall. Do an Internet search before purchasing.

CRIB BUMPER Fabric-covered foam-rubber bolsters, flattish, cylindrical, or wedge-shaped, to affix to the interior perimeter of the crib. A protective barrier between the NFU's fragile cranium and the crib bars.

CROUP The term *croup* actually refers to a group of symptoms rather than a single illness. Its characteristic loud, barking cough will scare the bejeezus out of you, and you will panic the first time you hear it. BCF. Typically caused by viruses (although occasionally bacteria and allergies fire it up), the condition is rather common and your doctor will advise you on how to treat the symptoms.

DIAPER Baby blotter. Cloth or disposable. On the cloth side, environmentalists cite the landfill tonnage attributable to disposable diapers in the post-baby-boom era. On the disposable side, many FPPs cite the superior absorbency, lessening the NFU's susceptibility to diaper rash. Also, with the advent of tape fasteners, the "errant safety pin" risk factor of spearing your NFU is eliminated.

DIAPER BAG Bag for hauling diapers, NFU toiletries, and other necessary gear. If you're uncomfortable carrying a pastel satchel adorned with teddy bears, use your gym bag. Hey, whatever works.

DIAPER CREAM — JOHNSON & JOHNSON'S, MUSTELA BABY VITAMIN BARRIER CREAM Yet another variation on baby-lube-in-a-tube, this version is creamier, less greasy, and sometimes mildly fragrant.

CRITICAL SURVIVAL TIP

Sometimes diaper rash can be caused by changing baby formulas or by a food allergy. Discuss this with your pediatrician and do *not* attempt diagnosis yourself. Some notable allergenic culprits are strawberries and tomatoes. Also jalapeño peppers. I don't really need to warn you about this, do I?

DIAPER PAIL (aka diaper disposal unit, DDU) Your NFU will go through a mountain of diapers and emit fumes that will utterly astound and mortify you. Luckily, advances in diaper-pail technology have made the disposal process easier. In the old days foul diapers would be tossed into an old-school diaper pail (a glorified trash can) or stuffed into plastic bags and thrown on the back porch for disposal later. (*Note:* The back-porch method is *not* recommended, as the stray noxious vapors may infuriate neighbors.) Now, however, there are several alternatives that are both sanitary and efficient. The DDUs vary in features and complexity, but the basic common premise is this: you stuff dirty diapers into the top of the DDU, which automatically dispenses plastic liners at the opening. The diapers are then sealed and stored in the body of the unit for disposal later. One example is the Diaper Genie by Playtex. The Genie has a clever bag cartridge that sits on top of the unit and dispenses scented sacks that seal the diapers in a hygienic sausagelike sheath. You simply remove the diaper from the NFU, open the lid, stuff the diaper in, and give a firm twist. The diaper disappears into the body of the Genie, and after approximately twenty-five diapers you pull out the linked "diaper sausage" and throw it away. The Genie works consistently (especially when directions are followed), the refills are easy to find, and the price is excellent.

DIAPER RASH A foul, insidious series of small red bumps and tender skin caused by chafing diapers, usually *wet* chafing diapers. May cause crankiness. May cause baby to be irritable as well.

DIAPER SERVICE A service industry for the politically "green" consumer who prefers recyclables to disposables. A diaper service delivers bales of clean cloth diapers to your door (folded for an additional fee) and removes the "used" and possibly fermented diapers.

DILATION The process of enlargement of the uterine gasket (cervix) in order to allow the NFU to exit the womb and proceed through the birth canal. Progress is measured in "centimeters dilated," with 1 cm signaling the beginning of active labor. Ten cm is the target number that must be reached before the NFU can be propelled into the birth canal. (Think rubber Cheerio inflated to the size of a jumbo Krispy Kreme doughnut.)

DOORKNOB COVER NFU containment device intended to thwart toddlers from opening a door and getting in (to the bathroom, say, and giving the cat a bath in the toilet) or out (of the house, say, and journeying forth on the open road). A variation on the old college dorm "oil your buddy's doorknob" ploy, the doorknob cover is a plastic faux knob that fits over a real doorknob. When the NFU attempts to twist the knob, the cover turns harmlessly while the door stays latched.

EPIDURAL A medical procedure performed to numb the FPP's midsection during delivery. A needle is used to insert a catheter in the FPP's back. (Yes, it says "back.") A drug is then slowly released via IV drip that numbs everything in the vicinity of the NFU's exit chute.

Highly effective, most women rave about the procedure despite the needle-in-the-back element. Be advised, there is the potential for injury or nerve damage.

EPISIOTOMY A medical procedure in which an incision is made in the FPP-to-be's perineal tissue to enlarge the outer opening of the birth canal when the NFU's head circumference exceeds the opening's maximum stretch guidelines. This procedure is performed with obstetrical hedge clippers. *Warning: Do not look. Turn away. Shield your eyes. You have been warned.*

EXERCISERS NFU gym equipment. A contraption adorned with a variety of suspended toy-type items to entice the NFU to reach, grab, and otherwise engage various muscle groups in activity. Develops hand-eye coordination.

FEEDING SPOON Utensils scaled to the size of the NFU's piehole, feeding spoons come in everyday models, plastic or stainless steel, and special-occasion sterling silver. Many have handles that are bent back to assist the NFU in gripping and also to prevent accidental eye-poking, as the NFU masters the art of self-feeding.

FONTANEL "Soft spot" atop the NFU's cranium. The skull plates don't fully fuse until the NFU is about a year old. If your drunk golf buddies approach your NFU, "Don't touch the soft spot, meathead," is the appropriate greeting.

FORMULA A liquid food used in place of breast milk for bottle-feeding the NFU. Typically manufactured, there are several types, including those based on cow's milk or soy milk. Some parents even manufacture their own formula to cut costs. Check with your pediatrician for more information. Oh, and it smells like feet.

GATES NFU containment devices. Frames with bars or mesh netting, adjustable to a range of doorway widths. Pressure-mounted models are portable. Once the NFU has achieved "stair awareness," a sturdy portable gate is essential.

GLIDER A type of rocking chair (usually shipped with a matching footstool) that "glides" front to back in a smooth motion. Has a narcotic effect on an otherwise inconsolable NFU.

GYNECOLOGIST (GYN) A doctor who specializes in women's equipment.

HIGH CHAIR Long-legged chair equipped with a tray in which the NFU is propped during feeding sessions. Available in a variety of styles, from wooden heirloom model with carved ornamentation to more modern chrome and plastic version. Ease of cleaning is a major factor to consider, as baby food can dry like varnish.

HIGH-CHAIR HARNESS Some NFUs don't take kindly to high chairs and may try tray-leaping.

Harnesses are available to restrain the NFU. Some NFUs don't take kindly to harnesses or restraints, and the result can be something akin to a bungled bungee jump. (Say that three times fast — about the time it takes for a determined NFU to go from docile and safe to wild and endangered.)

HURL Baby vomit. Actually, anyone's vomit can be classified as "hurl," especially if it leaves the nose/mouth region with any force. Babies can hurl with surprising velocity, especially if not burped properly.

INDUCING LABOR From the moment of conception, the FPP-to-be's body systems are all focused on one goal — birthing the baby. This is not unlike a NASA launch, in which all systems must be synchronized and coordinated, all mechanisms in optimal working order for the launch to be a go. A minor glitch in hormone levels or intercellular communication can cause a snafu, delaying the launch. In some cases, the obstetrician may deem it necessary to move a stalled process forward. One method is called "breaking the membrane." This is done with an obstetrical crochet hook and, despite how it looks, is a painless procedure.

JOGGER This is the coolest stroller model on the market. Designed with exercise in mind, the wheels are oversize and a brake is provided along with a safety leash to keep the vehicle and NFU cargo from getting away from you on a steep downhill slope.

JUMPER (clothing) A female NFU garment, a sleeveless dress.

JUMPER (chair) An indoor recreational vehicle for the NFU. Jumper chairs feature spring mechanisms that allow the NFU to move in a bouncy up-and-down fashion. Some also have wheels and bumpers, which allow the NFU to navigate the room while moving in a bouncy up-and-down fashion. The infant version of four-wheeling.

JUMPER (suspended) A fabric seat attached to bungee cords and a clamp that grabs onto the upper molding of a doorframe. This apparatus functions as a vestibular chair, stimulating the NFU's inner balance system, so if the grandmother expresses concerns that you're allowing the NFU to slosh his or her tender brain, you can mention the neurological developmental benefits of the apparatus. But BCF. If you lecture Grandma too harshly, she may not babysit Friday.

LACTATION CONSULTANT Member of the Breast Feeding Brigade (BFB.) Provides information, encouragement, and support for the breast-feeding FPP. (It's not always as easy as it looks.) She adjusts your attitude toward breast-feeding and expands your understanding of the true function and destiny of the female breast beyond your recreational usage. And she also lays out rules and protocol of public feedings in the event

your muscle is required. Here's the drill: If someone —
say, a maître d' in a four-star eatery — has the balls to
suggest that your FPP might be more comfortable
breast-feeding your NFU in the privacy of the ladies'
room, you smack him upside the head (metaphorically)
with some *education.* How would he like to eat his dinner next to a urinal? The FPP learns feeding techniques
that will astound and amaze you. There may be times
when the NFU is eating and you don't even know it.

LAYETTE The complete ensemble of clothing
and linens for the NFU.

LETDOWN REFLEX The process by which
the breast milk travels from some unknown reservoir in
the FPP's chest down to the nipples. (Ask your doctor
or lactation consultant for details.) According to some
experienced mothers, the letdown process is painful and
"feels like nails being stuck in the boobs." Letdowns
also lead to spontaneous leakage, so be advised.

MATTRESS PADS Moisture-resistant pads
placed between the sheet and the mattress, protection
for the mattress in the event of minor malfunctions or
catastrophic failures in the diaper department.

MOBILES Collection of NFU eye-catching toy-
type items, usually thematic, dangling from an apparatus. Depending on the model, a mobile can be hung

from the ceiling or attached to the crib or changing station by means of a clamp. Fancier ones may include a music box, which will slowly twirl the dangling toy-type things while plinking out annoying tunes. Mobiles should be placed beyond the NFU's reach to avoid entanglement or ingestion of small parts.

MONITORS Baby bugs. Electronic or battery-powered surveillance devices to track the NFU's welfare and status when you're not in the room. Monitors range from simple two-part radio transmitter/receiver setups to two-way walkie-talkie-style units to video-equipped kits. Check out the bandwidth — too broad and your neighbor with a similar model may bust you jabbering like a loon.

NANNY In-home child-care professional. Since Mary Poppins is fiction, background checks, impeccable references, and periodic monitoring are advisable. Can be found via referrals or reputable agencies.

NEW PARENT SLEEP DISORDER (NPSD) Okay, I made this one up, but it sounds legitimate. Characterized by lethargy, sudden bursts of anger, disheveled hair, and baggy eyes, NPSD is especially acute during the first three months, while the NFU is ramping up to a normal sleeping pattern.

NIPPLE CREAM Lanolin boob-lube. Suckling the NFU can lead to extra wear and tear on the milk dispenser, ranging from soreness to skin cracking to bleeding.

NIPPLE PROTECTOR Silicon-backed, soft-foam-lined mini-helmets to guard nursing nipples from friction and irritation.

NIPPLE SHIELD Molded silicon device with outflow holes, designed to shape and aim the dispensing portion of the mammary gland; also affords some protection from overvigorous gumming or gnawing by the nursing NFU.

INVERTED NIPPLES Like belly buttons, nursing nipples can be innies or outies. Innies make it tough for the NFU to latch on. Various remedies are available. Recommend that you do *not* put ice down her shirt to "make those suckers pop out."

NURSING BRA Industrial-strength brassiere designed to support the ofttimes hefty mammary glands of the nursing FPP as well as provide easy access for the NFU, by means of flap cups.

NURSING PADS Round boob blotters. Once the FPP's system is primed for nursing, which can take a few days, any number of stimuli (primarily, but not limited to, a hungry whimper from the NFU) trigger the hormonal response known as the "letdown reflex." (See "Letdown Reflex.") The floodgates can open, and rivers of breast milk can gush forth. Nursing pads fit inside the cups of nursing bras and catch the overflow. Available in washable cotton as well as disposable.

OBSTETRICIAN (OB) A doctor who specializes in the care of babies and pregnant women from conception through delivery.

ONESIE Short- or long-sleeved one-piece undergarment that stretches over the torso and fastens with crotch snaps. Similar to a miniature wrestling sling, the onesie is one of the more frequently used outfits.

PACIFIERS (aka binky, NUK, passy, screech plug) The pacifier is an absolute miracle of nature. Not only does it calm the raging screams of a disgruntled NFU, it also defies the laws of physics. The passy has saved this parent from certain nervous breakdowns during road trips, restaurant visits, and the final five minutes of the World Cup championship. Its design is simple, yet the construction is an utter mystery. The bonding force between the handle and the rubber nipple resists even the most violent gumming by the NFU and would not break even when wrenched mightily by a pair of electrician's pliers. (*Note:* Manufacturers recommend that you frequently check the pacifier for wear and tear, although this parent believes a nuclear explosion would barely affect the integrity of the damn thing.) My NFU recommends the NUK. While he is too young to verbalize the reason for his preference, he did revolt when a comparable brand was offered during a trip to visit the grandparents. This parent drove forty minutes to find an all-night pharmacy with the proper model — well worth it when the screeching was instantly quelled. Believe me, the NFU will not be fooled and is very brand-loyal.

CRITICAL SURVIVAL TIP

Buy ten pacifiers and stash a few in the car, a few near the bed, one at the office, one in the FPP's purse, and others around the house. Also send a couple to Grandma's, just in case. You will thank yourself one day.

PACIFIER CONTAINMENT LANYARD (aka passy leash) A brilliant device designed to keep the pacifier connected to the NFU at all times. A Velcro loop connects to the passy handle while a small plastic alligator-type clip connects to clothing, crib pads, car seat, or other appropriate surface and disconnects if jerked forcefully. (This helps prevent injury to the NFU.) *Note:* It is wise to wash the leash often (they are dishwasher-safe), as food, saliva, and other foreign substances gather and will certainly trigger your gag reflex.

PACK-AND-PLAY A portable, multifunctional, travel-friendly unit consisting of a foldable half playpen with a bassinet insert. Upper-end models have attached gear bags and changing-station inserts.

PEDIALYTE A "clear fluid" usually given to infants when ill or in danger of dehydration. Cleverly packaged to resemble Gatorade, but the taste is actually somewhat salty and foul. When thirsty, however, infants will drink it but may make their displeasure known with a well-aimed hurl.

PLAYPEN Recreational containment cube for the NFU, with mesh or net sides and a padded frame. Very handy for storing all manner of NFU recreational apparatus. Beware of allowing the level of toys to rise to the point that the NFU can climb atop the pile and effect an escape.

PITOCIN A synthetic form of the labor-inducing hormone oxytocin, it is administered to the FPP-to-be through an intravenous tube (the infamous "Pitocin drip") when your obstetrician deems it time for your NFU to be born and the natural process isn't proceeding up to speed. Be assured that this is not at all uncommon and is done for the health of the NFU and the FPP and not because your obstetrician has an 8:00 A.M. tee time. Still, there is some controversy among childbirth experts as to the advisability of interfering with nature, so do your research prior to EDA (estimated day of arrival, more commonly known as the "due date").

> **CRITICAL SURVIVAL TIP**
>
> Juiced by the aid of the powerful synthetic hormone Pitocin, the FPP-to-be's contractions will rev up significantly, not unlike a John Deere hauling concrete slabs at a tractor pull. As the contractions do their work (see "Dilation"), the FPP will feel as though the NFU has been transformed into an angry alien. At this point, the FPP may curse you, the doctor, all men in general, and even your mother. Do *not* take it personally, do *not* call her "honey," and do *not* laugh. She is surprisingly strong in this state and can strike like a cobra.

PLACENTA From the Latin word literally meaning "flat cake," the placenta is an ephemeral organ that springs into being at conception and grows along with the embryonic NFU until birth. (See "Afterbirth.") It serves as an interface through which nutrients and oxygen pass from the blood of the FPP-to-be into the blood of the developing NFU, and waste products pass from the blood of the NFU to the blood of the FPP-to-be.

PLAY YARD Portable NFU containment equipment — playpen, pack-and-play, or freestanding kid-safe fencing.

POSTPARTUM DEPRESSION The period following the birth of the NFU, usually several weeks, a time during which the FPP's hormones are in great flux. The emotional response to these radical hormonal changes varies greatly from FPP to FPP. If your FPP's symptoms include excessive weepiness or other indications of depression that extra TLC can't mitigate, consult her physician for advice.

POTTIES Miniature crapper. A potty can be a freestanding chair-type unit with an outhouse-type hole in the seat and a removable vessel — the "pot" — to neatly or not so neatly collect the NFU's waste deposits. Models are available to suit almost any decor, including diminutive plastic imitation toilets. Some potty models, like the Baby Bjorn Toilet Trainer, are scaled-down toilet seats that fit right onto your grown-up potty. Very likely, your toddler will let you know which model he or she prefers.

Note: Potty can also serve as a verb, as in "Oh, look. He went potty on your golf shoes." Sounds better than "the little sucker shat himself."

RAILING GUARD Bed fence designed for the post-crib NFU's first "big kid bed," providing protection against roll-offs.

RECEIVING BLANKETS Soft flannel or thermal dimpled-cotton squares usually in pastel colors, these are wrapped (the traditional term is "swaddled") around the NFU for warmth and comfort, and to disguise any flaws in diapering technique from the FPP. You can never have enough receiving blankets. They are among the most multifunctional items in the NFU's layette and can double as bath towel, barf wipe, or hobo-style gear gatherer when you can't locate the designer diaper bag.

SIPPY CUP A cup for NFUs past the bottle stage but not yet ready for a beer mug, sometimes with handles friendly to the grip of little fingers, sometimes with a rounded bottom to lessen the tipping factor, and always with a top designed to lessen spillability. The top may be inverted with a ventlike slit or turned out with a flattened plastic protrusion with holes in it.

SLING Cloth infant carrier, worn in front. For the NFU, a simulated "womb with a view." The sling has a very comforting effect on infants and can calm them when nothing else works.

SPLAT MAT Tarp, primarily for placement under the high chair or booster seat, to protect floors from the performance art of a self-feeding NFU.

STROLLER Outdoor wheeled NFU recreational vehicle with handles or handlebar for pushing the NFU around town. Available in a wide range of styles, sizes, degrees of complexity, and number of accessories, such as sunshades, hand brakes, and cup holders. Generally, the more accessorized, the heavier.

TEETHING BISCUITS As the NFU begins the lengthy process of "cutting teeth," he or she seeks items (fingers, pet tails, rocks) on which to gnaw.

Teething biscuits are specially formulated tough cookies designed to hold up under extensive slobbery gumming without excessive crumbling.

TOILET LID LOCKS At a year or so, the NFU may take to "testing the waters," as it were, with a variety of animal, mineral, or vegetable objects. Will a potato sink or float? Is the post-flush whirlpool powerful enough to suck a cat down the drain? Does Mommy love that sparkly green ring more than me? Be smart and plan ahead. Invest in a toilet lid lock.

TOILET TRAINING Housebreaking. A rite of passage that takes place in the toddler years; you have time to prepare for this one. Some NFUs take right to it. Others prefer not to. Be patient. Be encouraging. If verbal positive reinforcement doesn't do the trick, bribery with M&M's is permitted for every successful potty occasion. Your toddler may be very proud of his or her body by-products. He or she may insist on your inspection. Feign interest and pride and approval.

UMBILICAL CORD A thick, alien-octopus-looking conduit containing veins and arteries that runs from the NFU's belly to the placenta. The unborn NFU's supply line. Following the birth of the NFU, the umbilical cord is tied off and you may be given the option of "cutting the cord." *Go for it!*

UTERUS The muscular pear-shaped organ in the female reproductive system in which the embryonic NFU is sown and grown. To stay with the fruit-of-the-womb metaphor, during the nine months of pregnancy, it grows from the size of a golf ball to the size of a watermelon.

VAGINA (You spent the first nine months of your life trying to get out of one and the rest of your life trying to get back into another. Sorry, I digress.) In this context, the outer opening of the birth canal, a tunnel through which the NFU must journey in order to reach the light of day.

VIDEO MONITOR High-tech NFU surveillance equipment. Can be a simple countertop rig or a complicated ceiling-mounted security camera.

WALKER Training wheels for a toddler. A non-bouncy wheeled contraption with legholes in the seat, into which the NFU is inserted in order to practice the alternating bipedal movement called "walking."

YURP Not quite a hurl, a yurp is when the NFU ejects fluid from his mouth or nose. Typically low-velocity, the yurp tends to dribble down the chin rather than fly across the room.

DEBRIEF

SO THERE YOU GO.

I hope you found enough useful information to help avoid freak-outs and meltdowns.

As you travel down the path of laughter and tears (and occasional curse words), always keep one thing in mind: your kid idolizes you from the second she enters your life. What may seem trivial to you is huge to her, and your feedback, interaction, and attention are like oxygen; she needs them to survive.

You have the power to instill in her a sense of self-assurance and confidence that will benefit her greatly as a child and resonate throughout her life.

Just be there.

That is all.

Carry on, Dad!

ACKNOWLEDGMENTS

YEAH, YEAH, I know. This section can get really corny, but it's my book and I owe tremendous gratitude to plenty of people, especially those who have refrained from stomping my liver over the years even though I deserved it.

These words barely scratch the surface of my deep appreciation.

Special thanks and love to my mom, Cary Sutherland, and brother John Self for everything.

To John, Carol, Trent, Corean, Troy, Lori, Josh, and Jordan Van Dyke for their love and support and being extraordinary in-laws.

To Dr. Rich Viscarello and Shirley Griffith and the staff at Maternal Fetal Care in Stamford, Connecticut. True miracle workers and brilliant friends.

Special thanks to my agent, Faye Bender, at Anderson Grinberg for seeing potential in this crazy little book and editor extraordinaire Liz Nagle at Little, Brown for keeping me straight.

Big thanks to Chris Campbell, Doug Johnston, Fred Lark, Barry Sisson, Anne LeMieux, and Ted Buchholz for helping bring this book to fruition.

To my incredible friends.

To fathers everywhere who make the effort.

ABOUT THE AUTHOR

Scott Mactavish is a filmmaker,
a writer, and the father of
two very fast boys.

He divides his time between
New York City and Charlottesville.

He ain't scared of no stinkin' babies.